↑
Sand Point &
Woodspring Priory

KEWSTOKE

Worlebury Golf Course

Observatory

Quarry

The Hayes

Ashcombe
Wood

WORLE

Ashcombe
Park

Milton Road

Locking Road

Hornets
Rugby
Club

Leisure
Centre

LOCKING

Airfield

Helicopter
Museum

WESTON-SUPER-MARE IN WATERCOLOURS

Revisited

Rosie and Howard Smith

The Garret Press

First published in the United Kingdom in October 2015.

The Garret Press, 6, Stafford Place, Weston-super-Mare, Somerset BS23 2QZ.

www.garretpress.co.uk

British Library Cataloguing in Publication Data.

A catalogue record for this book is available from the British Library.

ISBN

978-0-9934072-0-8 (paperback)

978-0-9934072-1-5 (hardback)

Cover illustration: Laura, Knightstone Harbour, mid-summer.

Closing painting: Esplanade below Claremont Crescent.

Design: Colin Baker.

Type: 12 pt. Perpetua.

Printed in Great Britain by: Booths Print, The Praze, Penryn, Cornwall TR10 8AA.

ACKNOWLEDGEMENTS

Our first debt is to our designer Colin Baker who, somehow, has managed to pull our ideas and images together and set them out onto the page. Without his skill and good humour, this book would have been near impossible to achieve.

Thanks also to Kathie Barnes and Catherine Preston for patiently checking and advising on the text, and to John Crockford-Hawley, Sharon Poole, Chris Richards and Brian Austin who have always been willing to discuss aspects and particularities of Weston's story. Any persistent ambiguity that remains is, of course, our responsibility. Dave Priddle and John Manley helped sort out steam trains at Weston station while our son Sam made useful suggestions we might well have overlooked.

The original 'Weston-super-Mare in watercolours' described itself as 'an alternative guide' with a mission of opening up those aspects of Weston that were often unobserved and ignored. Much of the early work in that regard had been carried out by our old colleagues in Weston Civic Society, particularly Philip Beisly, Bob Smart and Martin Taylor - we remain indebted to them. The task of describing the town to its citizens and visitors remains much the same.

Weston is fortunate in this digital age to still have a vigorous local newspaper, the 'Weston Mercury', from which we have received much support over the years. So thank you to former editor Judi Kisiel and to her successor Simon Angear, who has the particular recommendation of being a Westonian!

This book is dedicated to Warren Storey

artist and teacher

CONTENTS

INTRODUCTION

A SHORT HISTORY

INTRODUCTION

The first 'Weston-super-Mare in watercolours' (2001) describes an elderly lady who had lived in Weston many years without ever managing to visit Anchor Head. How can that happen?! And yet, these days, Rosie and I often meet people who admit to much the same thing.

We both enjoy seaside Weston - we were brought up on it, and it occupies a fair number of chapters in this book. But Weston town remains undiscovered and, we feel, neglected - both in its Victorian townscape and its wonderful setting.

The text has been brought up to date and Rosie has created an almost completely new set of paintings - only a few old favourites from the earlier book creep in to make us feel at home. There are Special Pages and footnotes when a little more information is needed and which might arouse our audience's curiosity.

Anchor Head at low tide

Weston from the hill 1835 –
after a painting signed 'TC'

In the late 18th century Weston-super-Mare was still a small village tucked into the southern slopes of the seaward end of Worlebury Hill. Its small church and scatter of fishermen's huts looked out over a wide, sweeping bay of hard yellow sand. The hill itself was virtually bare of trees, given over to rough pasture and the occasional sheep, the broken walls of its hill-fort could be clearly seen. High dunes protected the marshy plain which lay to the east, with the enclosing promontory of Brean Down to the south. Out in the Channel the islands of Steep Holm and Flat Holm completed a picturesque scene.

As the century closed, visitors from Bristol and Bath, eager to try out the new 'sea bathing,' started to make the difficult journey across the Northmarsh levels beyond Congresbury. Fashionable folk were beginning to tire of the older inland spa resorts, and it had become much more dangerous to visit the Continent since the French Revolution.

In 1808 the Pigott family (Lords of the Manor since 1696) sold the fishing huts and accompanying land to Richard Parsley and William Cox - Weston's first developers. Two years later, by way of an Act of Parliament, the fishermen were out and the builders were in. By 1812 the town had its first hotel, described at the time as "a large and profitless inn." Imaginatively given the name 'The Hotel,' it later became 'The Royal' and the fishermen's shacks had given way to "a town of commodious and handsome lodging houses." In 1822 the first bath-house was built on Knightstone Island, and in 1824 the small, medieval parish church was demolished and rebuilt. 1841 brought the railway via a branch from the Bristol and Exeter main line. At this time the town was expanding furiously - from 163 residents in 1811 to 2,103 thirty years later. By 1901 it had topped 19,000, and a century further on the 2011 census was describing a population in excess of 76,000.

Following the erection of a pier on Birnbeck Island in 1867, a defining episode in the town's history was the construction of the New Sea Front. Building began in January 1883 and took three years, although in the October of that first year a great tidal gale destroyed a quarter mile length of the partially built wall. The sea wall is masonry of great quality - a curving configuration of local stone with ramparts which fuse with the high rocks at Birnbeck; it then bends around the hill to mould itself into Glentworth and Weston Bays, running out to the low wall following the sand-line south towards Uphill. No other event in the town has quite matched the self-confidence expressed in the completion of that sea wall - and the splendid seafront enhancement of 2010 confirms the original's enduring quality. It wasn't until 1904 that the Grand Pier arrived at its commanding position in Weston Bay.

By 1841 Weston had its own Gas Works and in 1853 a public Water Works was established - until then people had had to rely on private springs and wells or rain water collected and stored in brick cisterns under their houses. A sophisticated network of sewers was constructed. In 1901 electricity arrived.

For the next 30 years Weston consolidated its position as a seaside resort. Many of the houses which ran back from the seafront were built with an extra room or two to accommodate paying guests during the summer season. Everyone was getting in on the action. A theatre and salt-water swimming baths sprang up on Knightstone Island. The town sported two magnificent piers. Paddle steamers brought visitors from Wales, and trains brought trippers from the Midlands. Weston was also seen as a healthy place to educate children, and a large number of private schools opened to care for the offspring of the British Empire's civil servants who lived and worked abroad.

Development stalled with the First World War and only picked up slowly during the 1920s. Despite the Depression, the town found fresh energy in the late 1920s and 1930s with several high quality public projects - a glorious Art Deco swimming pool, the Winter Gardens pavilion and its adjacent tennis courts, putting green and rose garden, and the construction of the tidal barrier across Glentworth Bay to form the Marine Lake. All this optimism was flattened by the Second World War and Weston emerged in 1945 with a badly damaged town centre and a damaged idea of itself. Poor decisions by Weston's Borough Council led to the destruction of some of the town's finest buildings and incoherent planning undermined its character and atmosphere. Being Victorian just wasn't cool. Holiday makers left for the Mediterranean and Weston floundered, trying to make itself into something it could never be.

In the late 1950s the town began to expand eastwards, consuming the village of Worle in the process and forming the area known as North Worle. In 1970, the M5 motorway arrived and since then, rather against its wishes, Weston has extended into the south-east and is set to occupy Hutton Moor and encircle Locking village. The imposed County of Avon (1974-96) came and then went; to the delight of many who had refused to leave Somerset anyway. But the Unitary Authority of North Somerset has been a mixed blessing - Westonians continue to feel neglected and ignored. To some extent, the town is beginning to value and protect its Victorian heritage (despite North Somerset selling off its 1900 library) and to appreciate what those first visitors saw when they came here - a wonderful seascape and a comfortable environment: a really good place to live.

Chapter One

THE SEAFRONT -
GRAND PIER AND NORTH SHORE

The promenade, outside the Grand Pier, is always a good place to start. Over the years there have been many changes here, but it's still easy to understand what brought those early visitors: the enfolding rise of Worlebury Hill and Brean Down, Knightstone Island and the easy curve of the bay form a satisfying symmetry which can still be seen and enjoyed.

Bikes up! On the Promenade

Below on the beach, Mager's donkeys wait patiently for their young riders. Above, the Grand Pier faces the promenade in its 2010 reincarnation; for on the 28th July 2008 its Art Deco pavilion burned down in a spectacular and devastating fire. (See Special Page 'Grand Pier Burning') In just over two years it had been rebuilt, cleverly enlarged and, by retaining its corner towers, held on to the spirit of the older building. Indeed, this entire area in front of the pier has been refashioned in recent years. The former raised lawns have been repositioned and replaced by a wide, paved plaza (called Princess Royal Square) across which only restricted traffic is allowed. A high, sheltering semicircle of slatted stone shields a fine cast-iron fountain which has inhabited this area for a hundred years - it's now surrounded by a shallow pool, irresistible to children in hot weather.

The Grand Pier entrance (for a while there was a disastrous 1960s replacement for the Edwardian original) is now an energetic Disneyesque gateway. It plies a familiar trade of chips and candy floss - but I'm still waiting for the return of the pier's tooth-cracking toffee apples. I remember a time when you had to pay sixpence and squirm through a turnstile to get onto the pier. At present, it's £1 to enjoy the open walk along the pier-bridge with

Waiting to cross

the pavilion towering before you. This is where scenes from the film 'Remains of the Day' were played, although the cast-iron tracery of the original shelters has gone.

Looking back from the pier, the town acquires a fresh perspective. To the north; Weston is settled comfortably below its wooded hill, while to the south the vista stretches away; along the Beach Lawns and the sand dunes of Uphill Beach to the rolling peninsula of Brean Down. This is what the Victorians were on about of course; taking a trip out to sea without leaving dry land!

Meanwhile, the Grand Pier pavilion awaits with all the rowdy clatter of a funfair. It gathers you in! Shrieks from the dodgems, the whirling tumbrils of the fruit machines, the House of Horrors and Dead Man's Cove, a chink - chink - chink of the coin heaps, forever poised on the edge of delivering a cascade of wealth - which never comes - at least not for me. Swirling Go-Karts and Hot Flash. There is an inescapable urgency to it all. And there ever was.[1]

The southern side of the pavilion is protected by a huge conservatory with glass that opens up in sunny weather. Continuing on around the pavilion, Weston Bay reveals itself; not the full 360 degrees you had at the western end of the Deco pier, but a splendid panorama all the same.

Before going any further, homage must be paid to the town's Local Board who had the wisdom and courage to commission Weston's magnificent seawall. Built in the 1880s, it runs nearly two miles from the Sanatorium (now Royal Sands) to the heights above the Old Pier at Birnbeck. It is a formidable structure. Designed by T.J.Scoones and constructed by A.Krauss over about three years, it's made up from huge blocks of local Carboniferous limestone fashioned into a dramatic linear sweep rising high above the bay. Over the intervening years, it has resisted, just about, all that the Bristol Channel could hurl at it. (See Special Page: 'The New Seafront').

[1]In 'Cider with Rosie', Laurie Lee describes the pier's penny machines where condemned men are forever being decapitated, strung up or garrotted. Long ago I discovered if you peered through the gap in the gates of the model execution yard, you could watch the head pop up from the basket to reconnect with the neck! It was oddly reassuring. Some of these machines can now be found at Weston Museum.

The Grand Pier burning

I'd only ever known the Grand Pier in its 1933 rendition - a beautiful Art Deco hangar with
towers at each corner enclosing a noisy funfair. It hadn't started out like that.
Work on the original structure began in 1903 with the Edwardian Pavilion arriving a year later.
It too had towers at each corner, restaurants, shops and a theatre crowned
by a high central dome. Bands played and a wide variety of plays and theatricals
were performed including: Shakespeare, music hall and ballet. An attempt to cash in on Birnbeck
Pier's steamer trade failed after an enormous quarter mile extension beyond the pavilion
encountered dangerous currents and silting. The extension was removed in 1916.

In 1930, the pavilion was destroyed by fire - my father watched it burn:
"There was nothing left - just twisted iron girders." It's ironic, but that devastating fire probably
secured the pier's financial security for the new Deco building, when it arrived in 1933,
no longer housed a music hall theatre. Instead, the pier became my rowdy covered
funfair with a multiplicity of rides, a Crazy House and Hall of Mirrors,
dodgems and machines. The heart of the seaside town.

So when history repeated itself in 2010 and a probable electrical fault triggered a ferocious fire which consumed the Deco pavilion in a matter of hours - this time it was Rosie and I watching it burn. And it ended up the same as its predecessor: a heap of mangled ironwork - although the north-east tower hung on to the bitter end. The fire service did its best - the tide was out (of course), so huge hoses were rolled out along the prom to take water from the Marine Lake. Fortunately for the town there was no wind, so the enormous volume of smoke formed a great vertical column and disappeared above the bay. In the end, the destruction was confined to the pavilion area with the pier-bridge and wooden decking being entirely conserved. It later turned out that a major factor in the disaster had been the failure of the responsible security company to respond to its own fire alarm system.

Brother and sister Westonians Kerry and Michelle Michael, who had only taken over the pier from the Brenner family in 2008, immediately set to work on a major restoration. Bristol architects Angus Meek designed a substantially larger pavilion with a wide, wavelike, swooping roof but keeping the hallmark corner towers. The funfair model has been retained but the rides are now more sophisticated. The pavilion space is also more flexible and can be contrived to accommodate shows and musical performances - a touch of 'back to the future'?

Back on the prom and directly opposite the pier is Regent Street which runs into the heart of the town. The promenade road running north is called Royal Parade and displays essential seaside Weston: a collection of shops selling chips, sweets, rock (sticks of), ice-cream, buckets and spades and more chips - all accompanied by lashings of sand, sea and hot oil. A little further along, fronting the Crazy Golf Course in Victoria Square, is Fella's Ice Cream kiosk - a lone remnant of the many wonderful Italian ice cream 'Parlors' (Forte's especially) which made and sold ice cream before and after the Second World War. Victoria Square, once a small park, is overlooked by three-storey terraced houses - many subdivided for holiday letting. The Sovereign Centre shopping mall sea-front entrance forms the square's eastern boundary and its cafe has a fine view of the Grand Pier pavilion.

A short distance north of Victoria Square stands the low silver dome of the Winter Gardens Ballroom Pavilion with its latter day conference centre extending behind.[2]

Just beyond the ballroom, the esplanade suddenly opens out to wide lawns fronting the Royal Hotel with the Cabot Court and Grosvenor Hotels - the last two, a late Victorian development collectively called Royal Terrace. Sadly, some of this open space has lately been sacrificed to a cafe and car parking, but it remains largely green and uncluttered - a superb setting for the hotel buildings.[3]

[2]*The Winter Gardens ballroom, together with its Summer Gardens of tennis courts, roses and a putting green, was built in 1927. The atmospheric ballroom remains true to its time with a low dance floor encircled by a raised gallery with tables and chairs - from which you can watch the action. In the early 1990s, the tennis courts gave way to its conference centre extension. You'll find five Rosie Smith tile panels here depicting Weston's parks. The loss of the sheltered rose garden is still mourned. At the time of writing, there are moves afoot for the Winter Gardens to be sold to Weston College for the price of £1!*

Next to the Cabot Court Hotel, Knightstone Road joins the promenade and takes over from Royal Parade to curve north-west along the shore towards Knightstone Island. Across the road from the Cabot, on its landward side, is the Thatched Cottage: Weston's last thatched building and a survivor from village Weston. It was built in 1791 by the Rev William Leeves of Wrington for his summer holidays.[4] There was a time cream teas were were served on its sunny lawns. Nowadays, it's a restaurant and the lawns have been paved. Looking east down Knightstone Road, and dwarfed by ten storey Weston College, is the Lauriston Hotel for the Blind. Its fine main building is late Victorian but the house which forms an annex is much earlier. Moving past Leeves' cottage and around Victoria Mansions (a Victorian house of buff Bath-stone which was once the County Hotel), you come to two more two-storey houses with simple classical proportions - joyfully one still has its lawn and boundary wall. Deckchairs and lemonade belong here... and croquet with a glass of Pimm's perhaps? These two houses, which alone retain their original frontage, are part of a terrace called Victoria Buildings built in the 1830s. The rest of the terrace, although holding on to vestiges of their 19th century character, have all added a third floor and a jumble of sun-lounges.

Immediately north of this group of hotels lies the Melrose car-park named after an adjoining hotel - now the Old Colonial. This area was originally a shrubbery park that fronted Park Place - the row of large houses occupying its northern boundary. Amongst these, Park House (no.1) and Saville House (no.2) are visually unaltered. Also overlooking this former parkland on its eastern edge is Royal Crescent which, with its Georgian proportions and Bath-stone facing, aspires to grander things. Built in the late 1840s, the crescent was for years semi-derelict. It has now been splendidly restored.

[3]These areas of undeveloped land were a feature of this part of the sea-front until well into the 20th century. They were kept open by restrictive covenants protecting the sea views of various boarding houses. Among the last to be built on was the Winter Gardens site and, much later, the conference centre extension - both needed the agreement of the Royal Hotel to go ahead.

[4]Even in 1902, it was considered to be "one of the few remaining relics of Old Weston" - although by then it had become Reed's Dairy. In Rev Leeves' time the village ended about here with a rough track going on to Knightstone. It must have been an idyllic spot.

To the west of the car-park, what was (until 2009) a sedate putting green has been converted into a hugely popular Water Park for young children. This is an hysterical place of squirting fountains where squealing children get soaking wet with abandoned delight. Not a bad swap for a putting green, although the original residents of Park Place would certainly not have approved!

The western boundary of Park Place is formed by the narrow road Greenfield Place, most of which is occupied by Greenfield Terrace - rather more exuberantly Victorian than Royal Crescent. From Greenfield Terrace, a gentle slope leads to Upper Church Road filled on its south side by a curving terrace of small hotels.[5] In summer, their basement front gardens are chockfull of flowers and hanging baskets in friendly competition. Two pubs face one another across the street: the Criterion and the Raglan Arms (closed at the time of writing) which contribute to a real English holiday atmosphere. Behind the hotels and Greenfield Place is another redundant garden-park (now Hampton car-park) which the guest houses overlooked - there were once tennis courts here.

Back on the seafront, directly opposite the Melrose car-park, stands sculptor John Maine's enormous granite 'Weston Arch' rising a spectacular eight metres (26ft) above the road - although its impact is diminished by a clutter of traffic lights. It forms a gateway through the secondary sea-wall flood defences onto the promenade. Indeed, nearly the entire Weston esplanade has been transformed since 2007 when the sea defences were upgraded. (See Special Page: 'The New Seafront') This involved the promenade being paved in beautiful granite stone - warm greys, pinks and soft terracottas - set on a bias between the opposing sea-walls emphasising the pavement's width. The dull dead tarmacadam has gone, replaced by a wonderful, bright, reflective surface - sometimes it can be too dazzling! Huge quarried chunks of Mendip limestone are set into the esplanade forming seats and resting places, and where children can scramble and climb. Close by, a broken-down shelter has been rebuilt in Bath-stone as the 'Cove West' cafe - superbly positioned on the high seawall, its wide windows look out over the bay and the pier.

Beyond Greenfield Place and facing the sea is a further terrace of hotels echoing the pattern of Victoria Buildings, but this time named after Queen Victoria's husband

Albert. The terrace closes opposite Knightstone Causeway which crosses to Knightstone Island. Viewed from the esplanade, the island's buildings form a dramatic group whose profile has altered substantially since 2007. At that time, the original Dr Fox's Bathhouse, the Theatre Pavilion and the Baths (all closed since the 1990s) were restored and reinvented as apartments and cafes. In addition, a modest tower and further flats were shoehorned in around the site; so it's now a rather crowded island. In their prime, the baths were salt-water with the sea water being cleared in huge, subterranean settling tanks. Despite the changes, the island, along with the Grand Pier, remains an inimitable part of the town's seascape. Part of the development plan was to preserve the footpath around the perimeter of the island and walking the path still provides a great prospect of Weston Bay.[6] Knightstone remains a popular spot for local fishermen and, with a big tide, boats like the Balmoral and the paddle-ship Waverley are able to dock alongside the bathhouse for trips out into the Severn Sea.

Sarah and Daisy at the Water Park

[5]*During the 1940s, my relations Irene and Cyril Jackson ran one of the hotels called Florence House (it still is). In the late war years it was filled with RAF and American servicemen.*

[6]*There's a story that the name Knightstone arose from the island being the burial place of a Roman knight. When "human bones of gigantic size" were unearthed during early building work, it seemed to confirm the tradition. Unfortunately, they were carried off by "a man from Bristol" and never seen again. In 1822, the first open-air baths were opened along with various fashionable hot and cold seawater treatments. They even drank the stuff! Around 1830, Dr Long Fox of Brislington bought the island and converted the pebbly path to the island into a causeway. He built the handsome Regency bathhouse (which still stands) along with lodging houses which, in the early 1900s, made way for the theatre and swimming baths. In 1977, the baths switched from salt to fresh water - eventually closing, along with the theatre, in 1992. Within the 2007 development, where the Ladies Baths used to be, there's a courtyard with an extended tile-painting by Rosie (completed in the presence of the Queen) called 'Sarah swimming' which tells the story of the island.*

Looking to Worlebury Hill

Knightstone Causeway provides Weston with a sheltered anchorage and the area on its south side is known as Knightstone Harbour. This is where trips to Steep and Flat Holm islands run, with the wide slipway providing a takeoff point for power boats and water skiers. On the north side of the causeway lies the Marine Lake; an attempt to solve the disappearing sea problem by trapping the tide within a barrier (also a causeway) thrown across the mouth of what was once called Glentworth Bay. The 1929 Marine Lake scheme also involved the promenade being extended beyond the Victorian sea-wall to provide changing booths below, along with shelters, a ticket office and ice-cream stalls above. There was one very high slide, its top level with the prom, which thrillingly, and dangerously, shot you out into deep water. I was rescued once - dragged up by my hair! You could swim out to pontoons in the centre of the lake and there was a whole variety of boats to mess around in. And there are British Railway posters showing the whole scene in glorious Technicolor to prove it!

In 1981, an enormous tidal storm tore into Weston ripping up much of the sea-front including the Marine Lake's extended promenade, which then had to be demolished. This revealed the old Victorian sea-wall; not seen since the late 1920s. The tidal barrier survived the storm (it has subsequently been restructured) so the lake remains somewhere children can have sea and sand all day long. It's also an ideal place to catch shore crabs; dangle a line, with a bit of fish or meat attached, over the Marine Lake side and you'll soon have a bucket of seawater rattling with them. The lake's high, encircling, stone wall is wonderfully sheltering and this area of the beach is a great sun-trap. But when the tides are high enough to submerge the causeway, the Marine Lake returns to its original form as Glentworth Bay.

Back on the promenade, Knightstone Road continues around the Marine Lake to become Birnbeck Road. The three storey terrace facing the sea was originally known as Prince's Buildings - erected in the 1840s, it has survived with its 19th century frontage fairly intact. The restaurant/bar which now occupies the building on the west corner of Upper Church Road, facing Knightstone Causeway, was once the home of the Forte's No.2 Ice-cream Parlor - famous for its wonderful ices and glasses of coffee.[7] At the other end of the terrace stood Glentworth Hall, a fine house with curved gables and bay windows. It was sacrificed in the orgy of 1970s developments - its dull substitute block of flats doesn't improve with age. In contrast, something can arrive which immediately fits in. In 2013, a high conical helter-skelter, temporarily, positioned itself at the entrance to the Knightstone Causeway - a bright cone of red and yellow, topped by a Union Jack, which lifted the spirits with a racing spiral ride.

[7] *Forte's No.2 Ice-cream Parlor (they used the American spelling) was one of three Fortes establishments in the town run by various members of the same Italian family and open every day except Christmas Day, often until 10 o'clock at night. Immediately behind the 'parlor' was the ice-cream factory. It made ice-cream for the other Fortes in Weston and in the surrounding area. Many who remember Forte's ice-cream rate it as "the best ever!" Firm, icy crystals, creamy, not too sweet. Perfection. Even during the war, Forte's continued to make ice-cream "for the national morale". When supplies of pineapples dried up, Forte's No.2 contrived a replacement with turnip chips and pineapple essence. After the war, when real pineapples returned, people complained about the change in flavour! Nancy Browns, Eskimo Pies, North Poles, Knickerbocker Glorys... their coffee and ring doughnuts were pretty good too. It closed around 1970. Its big brother Forte's No. 1 on Beach Road had closed in the 1960s - although a smaller parlor on The Centre held out for a few more years.*

Beyond Knightstone, Weston-super-Mare's character changes. The town takes on a quieter, more reflective mood. Grand terraces form up on the hillside. Holy Trinity Church spire breaks the skyline like an exclamation mark with the backdrop of the woods softening the line of Worlebury Hill. Along and above the promenade is the convex curve of Claremont Crescent looking out across the Marine Lake to Brean Down and beyond. Stop below at the Cove restaurant for a drink or a meal (the fish is excellent) or above on the veranda of Dauncey's Hotel and contemplate, on a summer's evening, the comings and goings of the tide. Below the crescent, the promenade follows the line of the promontory, narrowing and twisting as seafront buildings crowd in, jostling for position. This is Anchor Head.[8] A small pebbled cove with great rocks for climbing and the sea close at hand. Keep it to yourself! You can stretch out on the warm sloping stone while children fish for crabs from the old slipway. A restorative from all this exhausting activity is at hand in the Cove Cafe tucked away above the sea-wall. Exquisitely sheltered, there's coffee or an ice-cream here on just about every day of the year.

[8] *In 1820, Anchor Head was regarded as "the bathing place appropriated exclusively to the ladies.*
Gentlemen are considered as intruders and will do well to avoid exciting the indignation of the priestess of the retreat..."
The latter being the formidable Betty Mugglesworth.

Anchor Head was once an important part of Weston's marine economy; its long, curving, 1887 slipway providing access, at most states of the tide, for fishing and excursion boats. It's also touched by history, for on 5th of September 1927, twenty one year old Kathleen Thomas made landfall here having swum the 11 miles (the tide-race actually made it twice as far) from Penarth in 7 hrs 20 mins. She was the first person to swim the Bristol Channel and there's a plaque on the seawall celebrating her achievement. The jetty still functions - just about - but it desperately needs to be cleared of rocks and properly maintained.[9]

Marine Lake, late summer afternoon – Louise and Fred

[9]*Despite the long slipway, Weston's tidal waters are challengingly shallow for much of the time and for this reason the Weston Flatner was devised - a flat-bottomed boat which could cope with most conditions. I can still remember when fishing was an important local industry with nets hanging out to dry along the railings of Knightstone causeway. Stall nets were staked out at Anchor Head and Birnbeck to become submerged at high tide. A great variety of fish was caught including cod, haddock and salmon. In season, sprats (a sort of very small herring) were caught in great numbers - so delicious floured, fried and served with fresh bread and butter.*

At Anchor Head

From Anchor Head, the sea-wall rises on rocky cliffs as the promenade constricts to a path around the footings of what was the Royal Pier Hotel (where the Beatles stayed in 1963 and where John Lennon told Rosie to "Go away!") - wrecked by a fire and then demolished in 2010. Steps lead upward, defended by a towering sea-wall, and then suddenly the promenade opens out again, with the vista of Birnbeck Pier (the 'Old Pier') on Birnbeck Island. This is one of the most dramatic prospects along Weston's shoreline, with the elegant, though now sickly, cast-iron pier reaching out from the hillside to the pierhead buildings on Birnbeck Island with Sand Bay beyond. (See Special Page: 'The Old Pier on Birnbeck Island').

Tidal escape ladder

    Above Birnbeck, on low cliffs, sit the lawns of Prince Consort Gardens and the elegant houses of Westcliff with their backs to the wooded hill. High up, a Victorian coastguard cottage gazes out from amongst the trees. (See 'The Hillside' chapter).

crabbin...

The Old Pier on Birnbeck Island

The Old Pier on Birnbeck Island

Birnbeck Pier, designed and constructed by the master pier-builder Eugenius Birch in 1867, is the only pier in the country that connects to an island. It is listed as Grade II* by English Heritage. The main 335m long structure (ie. the bridge) consists of 15 trestles of four cast-iron columns which support a continuous box girder carrying the timber deck. It was and remains a masterpiece of engineering. Most of the buildings (now ruinous) on the island are late Victorian. It became known as 'the Old Pier' when the upstart Grand Pier arrived on Weston's seafront in 1904.

At first, boat excursions from the pier to Minehead and Wales were rather ad hoc. From 1893, things became more organised when P. & A. Campbell ran steamers between Weston and Cardiff and beyond, and eventually became the White Funnel Fleet. Indeed, Birnbeck became such a popular destination for alcohol restricted Welsh visitors that many got no further than the pubs on the island itself! For many years a fully fledged funfair was established with some formidable rides. Campbell continued successfully until well after the Second World War, but by 1970 the arrival of the motorway and the Severn Bridge saw business fall away. In 1972, Campbell sold up and in 1979 the steamship Balmoral made its last call. From that time, the pier became increasingly dilapidated as various owners failed to make it work economically.

Weston's lifeboat has been positioned on Birnbeck Island since 1889 and there was a time when the entire town would be alerted by the explosions of signal maroons summoning lifeboatmen to rescue operations in the Channel. At the time of writing, the decay of the pier-bridge has forced the Weston lifeboat to leave the island and take up station in temporary steel containers above the Marine Lake. The island's fine 1902 lifeboat-house, with its long slipway and red doors, has been non-operational for some years. In 2005, a concerted effort by the Birnbeck Pier Regeneration Trust was thwarted in its attempt to buy and salvage the island-pier. The Old Pier still awaits its saviour but time is fast running out.

Chapter Two

THE SEAFRONT -
GRAND PIER AND SOUTH SHORE

Pier Square

If you're lucky; to the south of the Grand Pier entrance you may still come across a stack of deckchairs for hire. These are virtually the sole reminders of what was once a lively trade; a time when the council hired out chairs the whole length of the promenade. Working on the deckchairs was a popular student job during the long summer vacation and it's still fondly remembered - rather like Forte's ice-cream. The perfect summer job! (see Special Page) And it's here you find traditional Weston. In high season and with a little sun, it encapsulates the best of a British seaside holiday - a delicious combination of chips and vinegar mixing with the ozone, a bustle up and down Regent Street, amusement arcades, cafes and sweet shops. A drift of sand underfoot.

The Perfect Summer Job

You had to be well organised to get the deckchair jobs - or have contacts... I worked the Grand Pier Stack, which was almost hard work but friends, sitting in lone booths in remote regions of the prom, could watch whole mornings drift by without hiring out a chair. Trouble was, you could be sacked for falling asleep - on a warm dozy afternoon that could be difficult.

We had blue jackets with 'Deck Chairs' in red and yellow on the breast pocket - these became collectors' items. Because the sun always shone in those days and 1960s sun cream was pretty ineffective, I wore a lint patch to protect my nose which attracted a lot of Brummie banter. A friend of mine wore aluminium foil. He also had a huge khaki cotton coat (they had run out of blue jackets), dark glasses and a straw hat. His mother, sitting on the Sand Bay bus, refused to acknowledge him as her own when he tapped on her window. She needn't have worried; a few days later he was caught fast asleep.

At the Grand Pier Stack, if it did just happen to rain, everyone would pour off the beach and demand their deposit. Thousands. All at the same time. The promenade would be littered with abandoned chairs and windbreaks. It was a bit hectic for a while but afterwards you could be sure the rest of the day would be quiet. But then, of course, it could be very tiring staying awake.

All the same, since 2007, this area has undergone considerable change and what was an almost uninterrupted, mile-long sweep of the Beach Lawns is now obstructed by new building. Fashioning the plaza-square between the Grand Pier and Regent Street, has provided a wide and generous pedestrian zone, beautifully paved, where the occasional traversing bus or taxi comes as a surprise. The re-sited MacFarlane Fountain is a splendid centrepiece, with its encircling pond (often full of gleeful children) providing an introduction to the sea-front with just the right welcoming atmosphere.[10] Although it's no longer possible to look down the full length of the Beach Lawns from here, the glass-faceted rotunda of the restaurant 'Tutto' (now renamed 'Salvatore's') does provide a feeling of sheltered enclosure to the square. Beyond this point, the Lawns reassert themselves, separating the main highway, Beach Road, from Marine Parade which accompanies the promenade to where it ends, nearly a mile to the south.

[10]*The Boy and Serpent cast-iron fountain, made at the Coalbrookdale factory in Shropshire was donated to the town in 1913 by Thomas MacFarlane. It has now been beautifully restored.*

Archie seems to be hanging out with Ronnie these days...

In summer, the wide esplanade in front of the pier can be crowded with people waiting to cross over into the square and Regent Street. There's a friendly busyness about. An occasional roller blader/skater whizzes by. The "ding ding" of the land-train (like an old-style bus stop bell) and the warm sugary smell of candy-floss. Luigi's Rock and Sweet Shop beckons. Children hurrying by with buckets and spades, toes peeping out of plastic sandals, fidgeting at the traffic crossing lights. On either side of the pier entrance, wide inclines lead us down to the beach where the donkeys are patiently waiting. Shrieks as children bounce about in the saddle as their donkeys canter back to base. Again, if you're lucky, the sea will be coming in; sneaking under the pier when you weren't looking. The sea is warm. Walk out a little and let the soft mud squeeze deliciously between your toes.

If you've worked up something of an appetite; get a worth of whelks or cockles at the seafood stall. So good with a splash of vinegar and pepper! Sit on the sea-wall and let your fingers explore the honeycomb weathering of the capping stones - Rosie

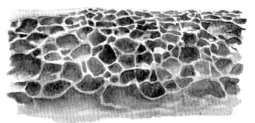

Weathered seawall capping stone

found a silver shilling here once. Hang around and Punch and Judy might show up. "That's the way to do it!" What more can you ask.

Portrait on the prom

Walking southwards across the square, the buildings along its eastern fringe await their own enhancement. The former 1930s Grand Central Hotel and Forte's No 1 have retained their Art Deco character, thank goodness, but many of the rest are neglected and sad. Circumnavigating the Tutto/Salvatore rotunda, you cross Oxford Street and immediately come up against new buildings that let Weston down badly. The first to arrive was Carlton Mansions replacing a handsome 1930s Bus Station. Built of brutal brown brick (brown brick simply doesn't belong in Weston!) and allowed to break a five storey planning guideline by rising to seven, it consequently overwhelms its neighbour the Grand Atlantic Hotel - one of the town's finest buildings. To complete the design mess, a Premier Hotel has appeared, looking like a blanched defector from the industrial zones of Titograd.

Despite its neighbours, the Grand Atlantic Hotel still maintains a strong architectural presence on the sea-front and is the town's only example of what might be described as a European Grand Hotel.[11] In recent years this section of the Beach Lawns has been occupied by various enormous exotic rides and carousels. Sporadically, a high Ferris wheel appears to provide incredible views over the town and the bay. The less said about its neighbour the 'Fantasy Pirates Golf Course' and its thudding ugliness the better.

Fifty yards south of the Grand Atlantic, we come to the western part of Ellenborough Park which serves primarily as a school playing field. The eastern section is a community park and open to all. Ellenborough Park, in its Victorian entirety, originally supplied the sea view vista for the grand homes of Ellenborough Crescent. The Crescent itself, built in the 1850s and faced in Bath-stone, aspired, like its sibling the Royal Crescent, to the terraces of Bath.

Ellenborough Crescent

[11]*Built as a school, The College, in 1854. It was converted into an hotel in 1889 with the addition of balconies and towered wings, and named after the transatlantic telegraph cable that came ashore close by. An early advert describes;*
"Pure air, direct Atlantic breezes, an inexhaustible supply of water and a rate of mortality of 9.6 per 1000."
Well, that's all right then!

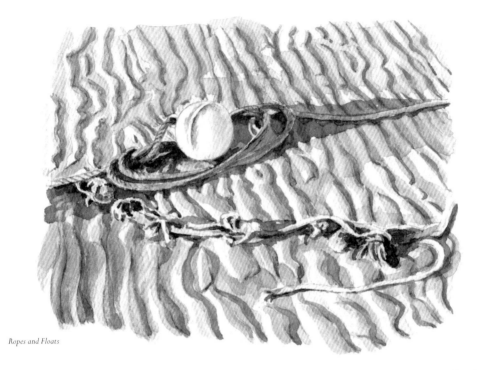

Ropes and Floats

Back on the beach, facing Ellenborough Park (and blocking its sea view), is the Sea Life Centre. In some ways this is Weston's third pier although it barely gets its concrete legs wet. Further south, down the promenade, is one of the town's real tragedies: the shattered remains of the Tropicana originally called simply 'The Pool'.

Up until 1983, this was a glorious Art Deco swimming pool a huge area of filtered seawater presided over by a unique and wonderful, arched and cantilevered diving stage. Weston is still pleading for a covered pool on this site. (See Special Page: 'The Pool.').

The Pool,
the Fountain and Banksy

During the inter-war years, the Pool was part of an exciting period of development in Weston which also saw the creation of the Winter Gardens, the Marine Lake and the Odeon cinema. Known simply as 'The Pool', its inspiration sprang directly from the healthful Lidos movement of the 1930s.

As with the Knightstone Baths, the Pool was sea water and it could be deadly cold.
The wide swimming area was gently shelving but just below the high,
cantilevered diving stage, it sank to a depth of 15 ft (5m) with a warning
of 'Deep Water'. From the 10 metre top stage (the highest in Europe),
the view of the town took your breath away - the Pool shrank
to the size of a postage stamp.

It took a lot of nerve just to jump from that top stage. I never did.
Even from the second stage it was a long way down and after you hit the water you just
kept on going. Forever. It even got dark - but perhaps I was just losing consciousness.
In summer, the top stage was raised by a further 10ft so that acrobatic divers
could leap after setting themselves on fire!

The Pool closed in 1982 and the beautiful diving stage, despite being Grade II listed,
demolished the following year - an act of civic idiocy. Its plastic replacement,
the Tropicana Pleasure Beach, succumbed worn out and tatty in 2000.
Somehow, through all the years of neglect and anguished debate, the Pool's Art Deco
fountain managed to survive - until 2012, when it was nearly decapitated while the
area served as a dumping ground for the seafront enhancement.

In August and September 2015, the Pool site became home to a
subversive but jocular international exhibition organised by the
renowned street artist Banksy. Over 50 artists from 17 different
countries were involved. Hugely popular, it was punningly
presented as 'Dismaland'; an anarchic 'bemusement' theme park of dark humour,
disturbing set pieces and art work describing societal breakdown.
To quote Banksy: "The fairytale is over. The world is sleepwalking towards
climate catastrophe, maybe all that escapism will have to wait."
Meanwhile, amongst it all, stood the broken Deco fountain:
redolent, forlorn, spotlit centre stage.

South of the Grand Pier, the esplanade is punctuated by a series of elegant Victorian cafes and shelters which are incorporated into the original seawall. This part of the prom has had to give up the granite paving but is rescued by streamlined, sculptured stone benches; their artist, John Maine, influenced by "the undulating curves of Brean Down". This area of the esplanade is wide and open, the seawall rising only a few feet above the sands.

South promenade

From Ellenborough Park, the eloquent though often manhandled Beach Lawns march south and where fine villas, standing to attention along Beach Road, have survived largely intact. Most new building here has been sympathetic and well mannered, reflecting the Victorian idiom and scale. These houses keep to themselves and their stately procession adds to the feeling of spaciousness of the whole bay. Indeed, should you come to Weston from the south to arrive at Beach Road; the unrestricted vista of the Lawns is unexpected and often quite dazzling. Looking north with the hill as backdrop, westering sunlight reflected from spires and terraces... the islands... sea and distant coastlines... kites, a cargo ship or two...

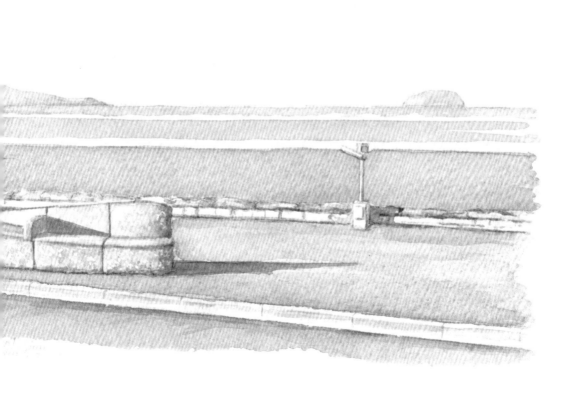

Kite surfing

    The processional villas make up the western boundary of Clarence Park which provides a sheltered retreat from the seafront. The houses eventually halt at the fitting finale of the gables and towers of Royal Sands - a development incorporating a former hospital.[12] Just beyond the Sands lies Weston Golf Course filling, north to south, the entire western length of Uphill Road North until it meets the small area of woodland which separates Weston from the village of Uphill.[13] On their seaward side, the golf links are protected by high sand dunes which once ran almost the whole distance of Weston Bay - to just beyond where the Grand Pier now stands. Although the promenade ends at the Royal Sands, the seashore continues as a wide sandy beach for nearly a mile, to the estuary of the River Axe emerging from below Brean Down - overlooked by Uphill's roofless St Nicholas Old Church on its 'high hill crest'.

Houseboat on the River Axe, Uphill

[12]Completed in 1868 and originally called the Royal West of England Hospital,
it was known to locals as the Sanatorium or 'the San.' It was designed for the treatment of illnesses
such as tuberculosis and Weston was considered to have 'a climate second to no seaside town in England'
for such curative regimes. With the arrival of the NHS in 1948, it was absorbed into the town's
acute medical care, closing in 1985 when the new general hospital was built at Uphill.
With new building, it now forms a group of apartments and houses.

[13]This wood, once part of the Uphill Castle Manor Estate, remains a defining boundary between
Weston-super-Mare town and Uphill village. It is now owned and managed by the
Woodland Trust which has also taken over an adjoining field on Uphill Road South -
see The South of the Town and Uphill sections.

The Royal Potteries

Sitting on an alluvial plain with the accumulated mud from the Severn Estuary, Weston had a ready supply of good quality clay. As soon as the town began to grow, a number of small brickyards were established: first at Uphill and later on in Weston. Brick makers were recruited from places like Bridgwater where bricks and tiles had been manufactured for many years.

In 1847, Charles Phillips bought the Weston-super-Mare Pottery in Locking Road from William Wilcox and almost immediately expanded the business, designing a huge range of garden pots, statues, urns and vases. In 1851, his pots received an 'Honourable Mention' at the Great Exhibition and soon after Phillips renamed his business 'The Phillips' Royal Potteries'. By this time, he was supplying Kew Gardens and the Royal Parks. Fired Weston clay had a quality that resisted disfiguring algal growth.

The Victorian period was one of active expansion and creativity, although after he sold the Potteries to John Matthews in 1871, Charles Phillips slid into penury, ending up at the age of 70 as caretaker of a promenade cloakroom, opposite the Grand Atlantic Hotel.

During the 1890s, the Potteries moved to a new site with fresh clay-pits, at the southern end of what is now Langford Road - where some of the brick sheds are still standing. At its height, the business employed some 150 people and continued, through various crises, up to 1961 when its fate was ignominiously sealed by the introduction of the plastic flower pot.

Innumerable Royal Potteries' products still survive: the pineapples above the doorways in Claremont Crescent: the White Lion in St. James Street: terracotta copings on stone walls and many treasured pots and urns in homes and gardens about Weston and beyond. I'm told there are still some Phillips' pots to be found at the Royal Botanical gardens at Kew.

Chapter Three

THE SANDS AND THE SEA AND THE TIDES

On Weston sands

Weston Bay is two and a half miles of sand and sea (and a little mud) enclosed by the protective promontories of Worlebury Hill and Brean Down. It is the central one of three bays, with Sand Bay lying to the north between Worlebury and Sand Point, and Bridgwater Bay running south from Brean Down to Burnham on Sea and the rise of the Quantock Hills. All three have superb firm sand where you can play cricket and slog a ball for miles, gallop a horse, run a dog, kick a ball, make a sand castle, fly a kite, sail a land yacht... In Weston, sand has a habit of moving from the north end of the bay and parking itself at Uphill - a process known as longshore drift. So, every once in a while, the sand is loaded into lorries and carted back to Knightstone.

Weston-super-Mare lies on the eastern shore of the Bristol Channel (the Severn Sea), the estuary of the River Severn. The tidal range in the estuary (up to 49ft/15m) is claimed to be the second highest in the world, beaten only by the Bay of Fundy in eastern Canada. It is also relatively shallow and this explains why the sea does its notorious disappearing act twice a day. The vast flow of water also explains why the Channel is favoured as a huge hydroelectric generator: the Severn Barrage which, despite its environmental dangers, may still have a future, in some form, when the oil, gas and uranium run out.

The New Seafront 2007 - 2010

'Tidal Enclosure' by John Maine

Following the ravages of the 1981 Great Storm and the further flood damage in 1990 and 1996, it became clear Weston needed sea defences that would cope with increasing danger - the beautiful, 1880s, Scoones and Krauss seawall had proved unable to resist exceptional storm surges. By 2007, North Somerset Council settled on a programme of seafront enhancement with Bristol born sculptor John Maine RA. appointed to oversee the design aesthetics of the work. Most importantly, funding was secured from Whitehall just before the country slid into an economic recession.

In 2007/2008, the Marine Lake causeway was raised, strengthened and also extended around the north side of Knightstone Island. Next came the installation of pre-cast concrete steps ('a scour protection apron') along the bottom of the Victorian sea-wall from Knightstone to the Grand Pier.

This was an enormous project - most of which has now disappeared below beach level. John Maine designed quarried Mendip stone blocks and worked granite to be positioned along the base of the beach wall on the protection apron. One, called 'Tidal Enclosure', at the foot of the slipway next to the Cove West cafe, is an eloquent seating spiral of smooth stone washed daily by the tides.

This section of work was completed in October 2008. Reconstruction of the promenade began in January 2009. This involved building a secondary sea-wall (the splash wall), faced with Carboniferous and Blue Lias limestone, capped with Scottish

sandstone (from Clashach), to run along the road/promenade junction, from the Marine Lake to beyond the Grand Pier. At intervals along the splash wall, floodgates are positioned to protect the entry points onto the esplanade. One of these, opposite the Melrose car-park, is marked by a monumental stone arch (erected in 2010), eight metres high and built of fifteen interlocking granite blocks. John Maine calls this the 'Weston Arch' saying it "mirrors the form of Steep Holm". The floodgates themselves are beautifully finished, often with stainless-steel fretwork echoing the ripples of silt, water and sand on the beach below. The gates themselves are hung on wide piers of fossil rich Portland Roach limestone. Storm drain covers are also fashioned from fretwork stainless-steel and, beneath the Water Park on Knightstone Road, a sophisticated drainage system has been installed.

For Rosie and me, the most affecting enhancement has been the granite paving of the promenade. Beautiful soft greys, buffs and terracottas; the slabs (from China) have been laid on the bias dramatising the width of the esplanade, with huge blocks of rough and finished stone (Portland Blue and Mendip Shipton limestone) pressed against the splash wall. All this has created a wonderful wide and, particularly for children, secure space - the single most creative improvement to Weston's seafront since the construction of the original Victorian sea wall. This imaginative theme has been extended to the spacious plaza in front of the Grand Pier and the smaller area above the Marine Lake - design and construction of the highest quality. It's a shame the paving runs out south of the Grand Pier - but be grateful it gets as far as it does! John Maine has placed sculpted granite benches at intervals the whole length of the prom, and closes with the most southerly taking the form of boats and waves to reflect "visually, the low sweep of Brean Down".

(Head engineers of the Seafront Project were Royal Haskoning with Birse Coastal as principal contractor. Weston-super-Mare specialist firm EJ McGrath was subcontracted to carry out the paving and fine stonework - a formidable task.)

High tide

At the time of the spring tides (when the range is at its highest, for several days twice a month) the sea comes in furthest and goes out farthest - almost slipping from sight over the horizon. But at Weston, when it's in and the tide is really high (say 42ft/13 m), the Grand Pier and Knightstone appear to float on the surface of the sea. If there is an accompanying onshore wind, the waves will be huge; crashing over the sea-wall with spectacular violence. On those days, and it's even more thrilling at night when the sea is really whacking in, there is powerful entertainment to be had. Running the curve of the north promenade, dodging the slap of the sea as it fizzes over the sea-wall, children set out for the inevitable delicious soaking as they 'run the prom'. They are even more delighted if their parents get caught by a rogue wave. Then everyone joins in, dashing up and down getting wonderfully soaking wet. In winter, it's even more painfully exquisite as the cold sets in and your teeth rattle in your head. Then it's time for a hot chocolate! The best places for these Spring Tide Specials are north of the Grand Pier:

opposite Leeve's cottage to Knightstone: the Marine Lake esplanade and particularly deadly: the section of the prom where it constricts at Anchor Head. All these vary depending on the direction of the wind, and be careful - at times the danger can be real. I've always felt the town should promote these bimonthly spectacles but it's another thing Westonians keep to themselves![14]

Storm drain cover

When the tidal fall is at its smallest they are called 'neap' tides. The sea doesn't come in so much - often barely kissing the seawall at Knightstone - but at the same time it stays in rather longer and doesn't go out as far. So in many ways the sea is more accessible on the neap. There just isn't as much of it. Neap tides are probably better for sailing and generally splashing around - the sea in the bay is also remarkably shallow. I remember a time in my youth when I was testing a rowing dingy with three friends - we had spent the entire winter sanding and varnishing it. We had already rowed out beyond the Grand Pier before realising the boat was filling up with water. We had forgotten to put in the drain plug! Alarm - Panic - Loss of all hands. Fevered rowing was to little avail... I decided to swim for the shore! - and on abandoning ship found myself standing in 18 inches of water, looking down on my desperate 'sinking' companions.

[14]*Spring tides have nothing to do with the season. They are the times in the month when the gravitational pull of the sun and the moon on the oceans is at its maximum - when the sun and moon are in line: at 'full moon' and 'new moon'. When the sun and moon are at right angles, the gravitational effect is diminished and we get the smaller 'neap' tides.*

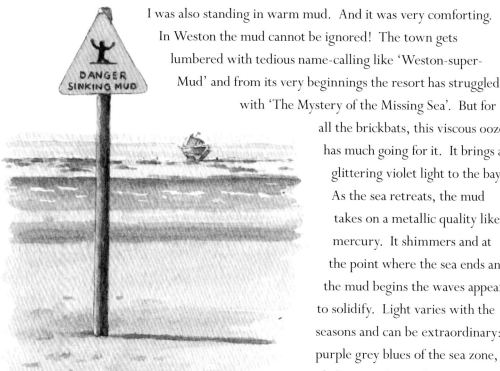

I was also standing in warm mud. And it was very comforting. In Weston the mud cannot be ignored! The town gets lumbered with tedious name-calling like 'Weston-super-Mud' and from its very beginnings the resort has struggled with 'The Mystery of the Missing Sea'. But for all the brickbats, this viscous ooze has much going for it. It brings a glittering violet light to the bay. As the sea retreats, the mud takes on a metallic quality like mercury. It shimmers and at the point where the sea ends and the mud begins the waves appear to solidify. Light varies with the seasons and can be extraordinary: purple grey blues of the sea zone, cobalt green skies, a lowering winter sun.

Mind you, the mud does have a few disadvantages. For a start, it can suck your boots off. It can lurk an inch or two under the sand and then slip like chocolate over your unsuspecting shoes. It's not a good plan to try and walk across the mud region of the bay - you can end up getting stuck and exhausted. The tide may decide to come in - and it will come in at high speed! Where parking is allowed at the Uphill end of the bay, cars that have driven out that little too far can sink up to their axles. Their owners then have to watch despairingly as the sea advances...

Weston Civic Society once sold Weston Mud. It was dried and packed in plastic containers. All you had to do was add tap water and you had the real thing in the comfort of your own home! The bathhouses on Knightstone Island also used it in various spa treatments and cures. The warm ooze that had so caressed my toes also soothed aching rheumatic joints and painful muscles.

Weston Lifeboat (B-769 Coventry & Warwickshire), Knightstone Harbour

The sandy margin where the beach fades into the mud zone is inhabited by many interesting creatures, but the most evident are the spaghetti sand hills of the lugworm.[15] Each squiggle of sand has an accompanying dimple, about an inch across, with a small hole in its floor. These mark the two ends of the lugworm's U-shaped burrow - a complete give-away to the fishermen who dig them up for bait. Fishing is popular both from the beach or from the heights of Knightstone and Birnbeck - cod, mullet, conger eel, whiting, bass: all provide good sport in their season.

Weston Bay has two main areas for boating. Knightstone Harbour is the mooring place for pleasure craft, fishing and motor boats. The wide slipway makes it possible to take a boat trailer right down to the water's edge, while the seawall quay allows larger boats to land and disembark. While Birnbeck has become non-operational, the slipway is also the sea entry point for the Weston Lifeboats. On a good tide and a sunny day, Knightstone assumes an animated Mediterranean air.

[15]*Lugworm (Arenicola marina) A beach may support over 13,000 worms per acre.*
They have a thick ruddy body with 13 feathery gills and a smooth tail-end - they grow up to 20cm (8 ins) long.
Each tide brings fresh sand to the burrow for the worm to ingest and cast out in ropey coils on the beach.

There are boats coming and going. Skiers whizzing back and forth. People peering over railings at excursion boats collecting excited children and parents for a trip around the islands, and the special occasions, on a really big tide, when the Paddle Steamer Waverley may call. Meanwhile, high above all this activity, others may be quietly taking tea on the terrace of Dr. Fox's Tea-room.

Uphill pillbox looking to Black Rock and Brean Down

The second boating place is at the southern end of the bay - at Uphill, where roofless St Nicholas' Old Church looks out from the sheer quarried face of Uphill Hill. At the angle of Brean Down and Weston Bay lies the estuary of the River Axe.

The Axe is a small but important river; navigable inland as far as Cheddar and Wells during medieval times. Its main function now is assisting the drainage of the low lying Somerset Levels, south of the Mendip Hills - land criss-crossed by a network of ditches and rhynes. At the river mouth, Weston Yacht Club has its headquarters and in a small creek, a little further upstream, is Uphill Boatyard and Marina. The enormous rise and fall of the tide means that boats spend a lot of their lives stranded on the river's mud-banks, but despite the tidal challenge this is a popular place for dinghies and various sailing craft - and even the occasional houseboat.

Surveyed by a shoreline World War II pill-box, Black Rock keeps sentry in the river mouth with its summit just managing to stand clear of the sea. The rock serves as an important navigational marker - especially so in the days when Uphill was a small port handling cargoes such as limestone and coal. But its role goes much further back; for Black Rock once delineated the western limit of the Forest of Mendip; an area stretching as far east as Frome, a hunting ground of the Saxon and Norman kings.

Chapter Four

BREAN DOWN

Brean Down fort and Steep Holm

Although it plays such a large part in the dramatic action of Weston Bay, Brean Down actually belongs to the village of Brean ("Bre-un" to locals). The estuary of the River Axe, which years ago could be crossed on a summer ferry, effects a real separation from Weston and secures the isolation of the Down.[15] The small road to Brean from Weston's A370 does much the same thing by wriggling a tortuous way across the rhyned levels, often travelling in the opposite direction expected, and adding some nine miles to a journey which, when you started out, appeared just a few yards from your front door!

Brean village itself is chockfull of caravans, but Brean Down is safely in the care of the National Trust. Having breached the barrier of mobile homes, there are two ways up onto the down: the steep stairway ascent from close to the beach, or more easterly and leisurely up along the old military road. The down rises to some 97m (320ft), an undulating cadence to the Mendip Hills with Crooks Peak away to the east.[16] Brent Knoll rises from the nearby coastal plain with Glastonbury Tor (misty Avalon) far off in the south-east. And then there is the sweep of the Bristol Channel, the islands Steep and Flat Holm, and to the north: the glittering expanse of Weston Bay.

The Brean Down headland is the longest of the three promontories (the others being Worlebury and Sand Point) which are such a feature of this part of the Somerset coastline. On the Weston side, it reaches out one and a half miles into the sea with accessible coves and gentle grassy slopes, bracken and windblasted hawthorn. It was on this side in 1867 that an attempt to construct a harbour was made. Ominously, shortly after the foundation stone was laid, both the stone and its marker buoy were swept away, some say to Steep Holm! In 1872, the partially completed harbour pier was smashed in one of Weston's Great Storms. The Brean Down Harbour Company collapsed with losses of £350,000 - an enormous amount in those days.

Brean Down from Knightstone Harbour

[15]*Gordon Gilham was the last of the Axe ferrymen. He operated until the 1970s rowing the boat and maintaining the walkways across the muddy river banks.*

[16]*Crooks or Crook Peak? The debate has been going on for a few hundred years! Locals have always called it Crooks, so it's Crooks Peak for me.*

White Rock rose

On the down's southern side there are steep cliffs which are recognised as challenging rock climbing routes. The climbs have enticing names like 'Torpedo' (extremely severe) and 'Cyclops Gatepost' (merely difficult). On these southern inclines and crags grows the rare and beautiful White Rock Rose (Helianthemum appeninum) - in summer the flowers appear to be everywhere, scattered like confetti. These days, you are likely to come across a herd of feral goats perched on the cliff sides. They were introduced by the National Trust in an effort to control the spread of scrub. On the western rocky outposts, you can find samphire; a succulent member of the parsley family and a gastronomic treat. Collecting it can be risky and Shakespeare has a character in King Lear describe its gathering as: "that dreadful trade".

From the Weston promenade, it's possible to make out Brean Down Fort with the naked eye - just visible at the tip of the promontory. When you've walked along the heights of the headland, a good mile out to sea, the barracks, gun emplacements and searchlight post are an intriguing resting place.[17]

The fort was badly damaged in 1900 when a soldier - later adjudged to have been temporarily insane - fired his gun into an ammunition magazine and blew himself up; taking part of the fort with him. What was suspected to be his skull was found some years later by a horrified picnicking party! The fine Victorian masonry of the barracks has survived and the National Trust, which has owned the Down since 1954 (and more recently the fort), has carried out an excellent job of restoration.

[17]Brean Down Fort is one of four forming a defensive chain across the Bristol Channel, the other sites being: Steep Holm - Flat Holm - Lavernock Point in Wales. They were built at the instigation of Prime Minister Lord Palmerston, in response to the fear of French invasion in the 1860s. Constructed to a very high standard, they were equipped with the latest rifled, muzzle loading, (RML) 7 inch guns and mountings. The defences were refortified during the Second World War.

Chapter Five

Steep Holm from its gooseneck spit

Gazing out to sea from the Weston promenade, your eyes are irresistibly drawn to the islands of Steep Holm and Flat Holm. Their names cannot be more descriptive, but all the same there's an apocryphal story of a visitor asking which one was which! From Weston's perspective, Steep Holm is shaped rather like a currant bun while Flat Holm is more a low Welsh cake. There are two other islands: Knightstone and Birnbeck, although they no longer quite count since they are now linked to the mainland by stone or iron causeways, and they are not surrounded by water at all states of the tide.

As a boy, staring out to sea through the cloudy lens of a promenade telescope, Steep Holm appeared a remote and mysterious place. No one I knew had ever got there or knew very much about it. When I did eventually cross that five mile stretch of water in the 1970s and stepped down the gangplank from the Weston Lady onto the pebble beach - well, it really was a bit like landing on the moon.

Steep Holm, about half a mile long and a quarter wide, rises 78m (256ft) above the sea. From Weston, we can see its small pebbled beach with a sycamore wood on its eastern cliffs through which a path zigzags to the top. Our view of the island is something of an illusion - it isn't shaped like a currant bun! We look at its widest and highest end from which it tapers away, like a teardrop, to its western tip - dramatic arches of stone known as Rudder Rock. The pebble beach slopes up to a quay constructed during the early part of the Second World War - it was built largely with dressed stone filched from the island's Victorian gun emplacements, when the Army took over the island once again. As you ascend the cliff path you come to the remains of the island inn. Thinking itself to be outside licensing jurisdiction, it was a place suspected of smuggling and carousing (almost certainly true) in the mid-19th century. Spoilsports from the Inland Revenue put a stop to that in 1885. Abandoned, for years the inn was a semi-ruin and the Army nearly finished it off when they blew it up clearing a track for a railway in 1941. Sadly, difficulties in restoration have proved insurmountable and it remains a romantic wreck. Steep Holm was an important part of Prime Minister Palmerston's Bristol Channel sea defences against the French in the 1860s. Six sets of gun emplacements were positioned at the island's west and east ends; crafted from beautifully finished Mendip limestone, they remain largely intact with their huge, 7-ton, muzzle-loading cannons lying close by. The Second World War batteries and searchlight positions are not faring so well with mouldering concrete and rusting ironwork.

Victorian cannon at Tombstone Battery, Steep Holm

Perhaps the most important thing about Steep Holm is its wildlife. In 1976, the island was purchased as a nature reserve in memory of Kenneth Allsop, a campaigning environmental writer, broadcaster and journalist. It is the

Wild peony, Steep Holm

home of the famed Wild Peony and other rare plants. It's likely that these were brought to the island by Augustinian monks, who founded a small priory high above the pebble beach in the 12th century, and grew them in their physic garden. The St. Michael's Priory site has been meticulously excavated by the Kenneth Allsop Memorial Trust which has revealed a complex and evolving story. If you're lucky, you may meet a Grey seal on the shingle spit or a Muntjac deer on an island path. There are cormorants nesting on the northern cliffs - and, in mid-summer, a few thousand perfervid gulls - everywhere.

Grey seal

The Victorian Barracks, now splendidly restored, sits on the island's sunny and sheltered south side, its terrace looking out over the wide sweep of Bridgwater Bay to the Quantock Hills. Nearly always that little bit warmer than the mainland, Steep Holm is the perfect place to explore and relax.[18]

[18]*The Kenneth Allsop Trust organises boat trips to Steep Holm,*
usually from Knightstone. The trips run from April to October mostly at weekends and
Bank Holidays and are dependent on tide times and the weather. There is comfortable seating in
the Barracks building where refreshments are available. The island has its own stamps
and other souvenirs. Check it out at the Trust's web site: www.steepholm.org.uk.
For a full insight read 'Steep Holm - the Story of a Small Island' by Stan and Joan Rendell
and their book 'Steep Holm Pioneers'. Rodney Legg has written a number of intriguing books on the island.
In 2006, Rosie and I produced 'Steep Holm Diary' telling the tale of the barracks'
restoration and various island comings and goings.

Flat Holm from Steep Holm's east beach

Flat Holm, despite having a different shape, has a similar history to its sister island.[19] It too had Viking raiders and itinerant friars, although no established priory it seems. It was farmed and, like Steep Holm in medieval times, used for breeding rabbits for their meat and fur - a coney island. Farming was relatively successful here and there were, probably for centuries, farm buildings of some kind on the island. During the 18th century the farmhouse was rebuilt and that's what stands today. It's a fair sized house with an adjoining walled garden, cottages and sheds. For a while, from 1884, the island was used for cholera isolation and in 1896 a hospital was erected - though hardly ever used. Like Steep Holm, Flat Holm has Victorian gun emplacements although the cannons were installed in protective pits.

[19] *'Holm' is a Danish word for a river island, a legacy from Viking times -
particularly the 10th century, when the Holms were used as secure bases from which to raid the mainland.
These days Steep Holm is under North Somerset jurisdiction, Flat Holm under South Glamorgan.
Visits to Flat Holm are usually achieved from Cardiff with occasional trips from Weston.*

For all that, what really distinguishes Flat Holm is its lighthouse. In the early 1700s several attempts to establish a light were refused until 1736 when a ship was wrecked near the Holms with the loss of 60 soldiers. This tragedy spurred fresh action and in 1737 a tower was built topped by a coal-fired brazier. Close by, to the north-west of Flat Holm, are some deadly rocks known as 'The Wolves'. It was here in 1817, the 'William and Mary' sank and this time 40 people drowned. This brought about alterations to the stone tower and by 1820 a fixed, oil-burning white light was installed. Since

The Lighthouse, Flat Holm

then, advancing technology has improved the light output - nowadays the light has a flashing pattern of white and red three times every ten seconds. In May 1988, the three lighthouse keepers left the island for the last time and the light became fully automatic.

On foggy nights the light would be of little use and then a powerful foghorn would be sounded. It was a noise once familiar to everyone in Weston. On such nights I remember being tucked up in bed on Worlebury and listening to the visceral, stentorian blasts - they sounded like a forsaken leviathan, far out at sea. It was a thrilling, dangerous noise and I would pull the blankets a little further over my head.

Paddle steamer 'Waverley' from Steep Holm's south terrace

Chapter Six

THE TOWN - PART 1

Weston Deco – Regent street / High Street junction

Returning to the Grand Pier and walking eastwards down Regent Street, surrounded by the chatter and clatter of the machine arcades, the first substantial road you come to is St. James Street on your right. This was once home to 'Fish and Chip' shops like Farr's, Coffin's and The Continental which have now given way to restaurants specialising in Italian, Greek and Asian food.[20] Fortunately, Weston still has plenty of fish and chip shops both on the seafront and in the town proper.

[20]*One Italian restaurant (dear to our hearts) in St. James Street has been present many years. Tarantella's (originally Pescara's and then Ferrari's) started life in the 1930s as a cafe run by the Sidoli family, later becoming The Continental Fish and Chip Restaurant. Italian cuisine moved to the top of the menu in the 1970s when the restaurant (renamed Pescara's) was taken on by Pasquale and Rosa (nee Sidoli) Ferrari - their wonderful pizzas and ravioli (in a 'furious' tomato sauce!) were to die for. Pasquale had been a PoW at Yatton during the war. After Pasquale died in 1991, the business was run in the same tradition by sons Mario and Remo who later sold it to an equally enthusiastic Italian family: Franco and Liz Ronaldi. Franco died in 2013.*

In many ways, St. James Street represents a lost opportunity. Not so long ago, it was still a charming mix of cottage shops and Edwardian frontages - most now lost. But there is one survivor: jeweller Leonard Couch at no.7, which has been there since 1896! And it's cheering you can still buy a lardy cake at Hill's Bakery and splendid pizzas at Tarantella's. Richmond Street, a small road running from St. James Street to the promenade plaza, is perfectly aligned on Steep Holm sitting full square on the western horizon and always something of a surprise. While to the south, St. James Street looks across Oxford Street to what was Dolphin Square - demolished at the time of writing and awaiting redevelopment. The hard lines of the 1960s square were always at odds with the 19th century character of this part of Weston - which is still there, just about, if you look above the ground floor shop fronts.[21]

Cecil Walker – Post Office Road

[21]*The creation of Dolphin Square in 1961 came about through the destruction of a residential community centred around Carlton Street. Terrace cottages, houses and an attractive small square were lost despite fierce local protest. The same sorrow is not being expressed over the demise of Dolphin Square.*

Regent Street itself houses the unsympathetic rear extension of Marks & Spencer. Next door, on the north side, stands the Burton's Building, only recently abandoned by its namesake - it's now occupied by Costa Coffee. The building is a wonderful expression of the Jazz Age with a cream Art Deco facade of columns, zigzags and elephant heads that wraps itself round into the High Street. In many ways, the coffee shop suits it very well. On the opposite side of the road, Barclay's Bank inhabits an old Wesleyan chapel. The intersection of Regent Street and the High Street (now marked by a curious inverted 'parsnip' with a steeple of flashing lights) defines two distinct eras. To the south, the buildings are largely post-war and have an unlovely severity, although tree planting and widening the pavements has helped to soften the street's unfriendliness. To the north, it is quite different as the High Street describes a gentle oscillation following the line of the original village street. The shops , mostly three storied, are an attractive, shuffled pack of early and late Victoriana, Art Deco, a former chapel (once Woolworth's, now The Pound Shop) and a few post-war rebuilds and insertions. This section of the High Street is a car-free zone.

Midway is the main entrance to the Sovereign Centre: a covered shopping mall with a glazed atrium at its heart. Its scale fits in comfortably with the rest of the High Street and it's a successful mixture of shops and restaurants with see-through lifts and about 900 car-parking spaces. It also provides an imaginative electric scooter scheme for the disabled and a protected way through to the promenade. Enjoyed by young and old, who will be found waiting in hushed expectation, is the animated clock - its robotic band gradually unveiling itself on the quarter hours to climax in a strumming, tooting, drumming grand finale on the hour.

The Sovereign Centre's atrium runs through to its north entrance behind the Italian Gardens at the end of the main High Street. Now known as the Town Square, this area has suffered multiple assaults in recent years with thoughtless management and poverty stricken landscaping. (It's painful to recall the lawns, the tennis courts, the rose garden of the original Winter Gardens) Meanwhile, the 1930's Italian Gardens soldier on, a pleasing formality of stone seating and statuary where the High Street takes a breather, the sea just over the shoulders of the Winter Gardens and close by two of Weston's oldest shops - Cecil Walker: men's clothing and now ladies too, and Walker & Ling: drapers and much else besides - weathering the vicissitudes of the internet age.[22]

The High Street now intersects with South Parade (west) and Waterloo Street (east) - the latter running through to the Boulevard: Weston's principal thoroughfare. South Parade, at first and second storey level displays its early 19th century townhouse origins - still largely intact. The parade ends facing the Royal Hotel (the town's first hostelry) with a wonderful Italianate Bath-stone building, once home to the National & Westminster Bank.[23] Next to the bank stands The Imperial, formerly The Bath Hotel, from whose balcony Returning Officers would declare the results of elections.

[22]*This part of Weston was badly damaged during the last war - especially that part of the High Street facing the Italian Gardens. You will see this is mainly 1960's rebuild. The town never quite got over the loss of Lance & Lance, a John Lewis department store, which occupied all of the Waterloo Street/High Street corner site. Four businesses, 'Cecil Walker', 'Rossiter & Sons,' 'Greenslade & Co.' and 'Walker and Ling' are the last, long established, local firms to remain in the High Street. Cecil Walker's attractive shop was part of the entrance to the Royal Arcade in Post Office Road, a passageway of shops that ran through to Regent Street. The arcade was largely lost to incendiary bombs - what survived later made way for the Sovereign Centre - the return of Cecil Walker's window is the sole remaining fragment.*

[23]*This is the 'large and profitless inn' described in the introductory 'A Short History'. It opened and closed a number of times between 1805 and 1815. So uncertain were its finances, whenever beer was delivered from Worle a bell was rung to announce its arrival! It was later enlarged and its companion Royal Terrace (now the Grosvenor and the Cabot Court Hotels) built in the 1890s. They are fine buildings with classical details: arched windows, verandas and balconies, set in their own tennis lawns stretching down to the sea.*

Standing on the pavement opposite the Royal Hotel, you are immediately aware of Weston College. Its seven storey bulk is quite out of scale with this part of the Victorian town. The late 1990s extension along Knightstone Road has improved things a little by returning the building to the street, with repainting and new windows easing the overwhelming concrete brutalism of the original structure.[24]

The High Street, north of the Waterloo Street junction, feels constricted after the open spaces of the Italian Gardens and its fine, four storey buildings proceed all the way to Grove Park - relieved admittedly by the high backdrop of trees on Worlebury Hill. It contains two of the town's oldest pubs: The London and The Britannia. The London was the scene of the sad murder of Ann Fisher by her husband Joel in 1844. Joel was publicly hanged in Taunton.[25]

The London is much altered since Joel Fisher's time but The Britannia ('the Brit'), with its own courtyard alleyway, is tucked away from the hurly-burly of the street and has managed to hold onto its 19th century character. The high buildings which proceed north from the Britannia have elaborately worked Bath-stone facades designed by Hans Price. Interposed is the 1960s frontage of the Playhouse theatre - the original, destroyed by fire in 1964, was set back from the road to form a small covered square, busy with stalls and small shops. The present theatre has a very comfortable galleried auditorium holding around 700 people. Opposite the Britannia, West Street runs seawards to meet the old stable block of the Royal Hotel. In village Weston this was West Lane and although war damage has meant some rebuilding, it has managed to retain its intimacy. Shops along its narrow south pavement are especially attractive: carved animal heads above a former butcher's and a trio of arches forming the windows of another. Sadly, Astill's Bakery on the north side closed in 2011, but there's comfort at the seasidey 'Cafe la Mer' (with its wonderful 50s frontage) resolutely offering 'traditional fayre' since 1963.[26]

[24]*In the mid-1960s, Somerset County Council pushed through the design in the face of considerable opposition. The Council declared it would provide 'a really vigorous piece of punctuation'. Good grief!*

[25]*See Brian Austin's full account in his 'Tales of Old Weston, Volume 2'.*

Wadham Street, which runs north from West Street to Grove Park, has also managed to hold onto its early buildings. Weston Civic Society spent much of the 1980s here restoring the large, redbrick, Victorian stables and workshops along the east side. For some years this became the Society's Heritage Centre with a restaurant, exhibitions and offices. The Civic Society has now repositioned itself at the Town Quarry in South Road but the excellent restaurant survives ('The Heritage') and Badger House, as the building is now called, serves many community activities. On the west side of the street, the run of former shop fronts and a pub ends at 'The Blakehay': an Arts and Community Centre, formerly a Baptist church and schoolhouse rescued from demolition by the Weston Building Trust. It now has an auditorium holding about 200 people, as well as meeting and studio rooms. In 2004, The Blakehay was taken over by the Weston-super-Mare Town Council. (See Special Page)

[26]*Since the 1980s, Weston has lost most of its family bakeries: Passmore's at Bournville,*
Durston's of Milton Road, Nan's of Orchard Street...
Winnie's in the High Street (for sourdough bread) and Hill's in St James Street (lardy cakes!)
keep baking, while Iris Hogg's Whitecross Bakery still makes wonderful bread; particularly
(for me) its corn loaf and its pain honore (a seeded, malty bread).
A branch of the Astill family bakery survives in Worle - and has started supplying
bread to the 'Food Den' delicatessen in West Street.
Hurrah!

The Blakehay,
Arts and Community Centre

In 1986, the former Baptist church, schoolhouse and manse in Wadham Street came under threat of demolition. The Hans Price building had suffered severe bomb damage during World War II and here it was likely to be completely levelled! The Weston Building Trust (an independent scion of Weston Civic Society) was able to raise the funds and the mortgage to buy all three buildings and set about converting them into an Arts Centre which it was later to call 'The Blakehay'.[27] The church was remodelled as a theatre with a raked auditorium (and, as it turned out, great acoustics) holding about 200 seats with dressing rooms to the rear. The schoolhouse became a cafe/meeting room on the ground floor with a studio theatre above. As well as this, the church frontage was refashioned to Hans Price's 1862 design. For a while, the former manse served as offices but after a few years, reluctantly, had to be sold to raise further funds.

Some of the original drive to save the buildings had come from the need to provide a homeless Weston Youth Orchestra with storage facilities and a place to rehearse and perform - it was to remain based at the Blakehay for many years. Weston College also use the auditorium for dance and drama, and the studio for life drawing. The concert hall is used regularly for theatre and public meetings.

In 2004, the Weston Building Trust was delighted to sell The Blakehay to the Weston -super-Mare Town Council which has subsequently gone ahead with considerable further improvements. The old church buildings now serve the town as a splendid cultural centre - just as it was originally hoped for and imagined.

[27] *The word 'Blakehay' was originally attached to an area of land lying between Wadham Street and Grove Park. It stands for a fenced area of dark soil probably arising from long cultivation. ('blake': black and 'hay': a hedge or fence) See Philip Beisly's 'Weston-super-Mare - Past'.*

Blakehay buildings, Wadham Street

Lovers' Walk links Grove Park to Lower Church Road where a Hans Price's masterpiece, the School of Science and Art, faces us. Price's use of glazed terracotta panels, high studio windows and carved stone is typical of the Arts and Crafts movement of late Victorian England. Yet, despite being such a strong and individual building, it is almost overwhelmed by its towering 1960s progeny: Weston College.

The old School of Science and Art

To the north of Lovers' Walk, on a bluff above the tennis courts (courts once under threat of being turned into a car-park extension), stands the parish church of St. John the Baptist and just below to the east, its former rectory: the Glebe House.[28] In 1824, the 13th century church was considered too small and mean to satisfy Weston's burgeoning population so it was pulled down and replaced by the present building. Even at the time, Weston losing its medieval church was felt to be "unworthy" and the new building judged one of " the most raw, wretched, discreditable specimens of Christian architecture". A little harsh maybe, but the town had lost an important connection with its past. Meanwhile, bits of the old church were being carted off and incorporated into secular buildings around the town - some getting as far as gateposts in Worle! Directly opposite St. John's is the stately Bath-stone facade of Oriel Terrace gently descending the hill. It has a discreet, lightness of touch which complements the church perfectly - it's good to see gate pillars and boundary walls gradually being restored here. Across the road from Lovers' Walk runs South Terrace which meets up with Royal Crescent and Park Place - already

described in Chapter 1. Along its north side is a quiet terrace of Bath-stone houses with tiny, sunny, front gardens. The seaward side of South Terrace has some very early seaside residencies (Park Villas which front a lane from the seafront: Victoria Walk) and then - lo and behold! - at no. 7 (Oriel Lodge) some of the windows look decidedly ecclesiastical. Their carved stone lintels were recycled from the old church!

Standing at the southern end of Royal Crescent and looking across the former parkland of Park Place (now a 'Pay & Display' carpark), you long for the judicious landscaping which would restore the setting of some of the town's best buildings.

Stone lintel, South Terrace

[28]*The Glebe House dates back to, at least, the mid-17th century although it has been much altered over the years. It's known that royalist Rector Christopher Sadbury locked up unruly villagers in the house during the Civil War. In 1790, a hundred years after the Pigott family acquired the Manor, a younger son, Rev. Wadham Pigott, was curate at the parish church. It was probably he who set in train the improvements to Grove Cottage and the Glebe House to accommodate his artistic friends.*

Chapter Seven

THE TOWN - PART 2

The Weston & Somerset Mercury Building

The corner where the High Street and
Waterloo Street meet must be amongst the
windiest places in Weston. You are either battling
against prevailing westerlies to get into the High
Street or leaving it blown inside out - along with
your umbrella. The broad pavement on the south
side of Waterloo Street was part of an early road
widening scheme which, mercifully, never came

to be. All this area was once filled by the long lamented Lance & Lance (of John Lewis)
department store bombed in 1942. One shop here, Leaver's, a family run hardware
and ironmongers since 1886, is sadly soon to close. The original shop was at
36 High Street - where, as I recall it, the back of the shop seemed to go on forever.

Waterloo Street, from Leaver's onwards, returns to the original building line
until it opens out onto the Boulevard. The south side buildings are three storeys high,
mostly faced in Bath-stone with ogee detailing above the first floor windows - there's
even a niche for a statue which went missing but is now back in the shape of a friar
burdened with some heavy beads - or foreshortened sausages. Meanwhile, down at
street level, customers wait expectantly for Papa's very delicious fish and chips. The
terrace concludes with Hans Price's extraordinary baroque confection: the Weston
Mercury office.[29] This wonderful building just shows the Victorians really did have
a sense of humour! The Mercury's balconied tower is now only palely echoed on the
opposite side of the road by the Constitutional Club's decapitated castle. This former
masonic lodge was originally topped by a striking half-timbered turret. The turret
was forfeited by neglect in 1981. So the Boulevard lost its Grand (and delightfully
crazy) Entrance.

[29]The Weston Mercury, the town's newspaper, remained in local family control until the 1980s, losing its own printing
presses not long after. It started out in 1843 as a monthly news-sheet called 'The Westonian' produced by Mr. James Dare.
His hand printing press can be seen at Weston Museum. From 1845, it had a keen rival: the 'Weston Gazette'
printed in Wadham Street. The two papers frequently took up opposing political positions, often alternating
from one side to the other! They merged in 1951. English Heritage describes Hans Price's Mercury building
as "Dutch Baroque with a dash of Spanish influence in the tower"!

Boulevard café

In spite of that, the Boulevard remains dramatically different from other streets in the town. It was here that John Wadham Smyth-Pigott, Lord of the Manor, had a particular plan. He loved Paris and it was on his insistence this road reflected that city's wide straight avenues. It was aligned on the spire of Christ Church rising from the Montpelier hillside, making a splendid finale to the gabled prospect of the tree lined street. It remains a fine road with generous pavements, ideal for street cafes, even though the view of Christ Church has been marred by the intrusion of a pair of 1960s semi-detached houses.[30]

[30]*The Boulevard was originally planted with a mixture of elms and London planes. In the 1950s, the Parks Department took it upon itself to replace them with Japanese cherries - I remember the felling of those trees as I walked to Christ Church School. The Kanzan cherry blossom is a blowsy show for a week or two in spring - if the wind is kind - but the trees are poorly shaped and sickly for the rest of the year. As they died, they were replaced with native cherries and small-leafed ash. Recently, the Kanzan cherries are staging a comeback as replacements for lost trees.*

The south side of the Boulevard, along its westerly third, has undergone considerable change in the recent past with the loss of many local businesses. Especially missed is Weston Decorators (which supplied just about everything for garden and home) whose 1880 iron and terracotta frontage is now part filled by a Tesco Express store. Some of the buildings here have elaborate gable ends betraying an Arts and Crafts influence. A former photographic studio, next to the Mercury office, has high north-facing windows. These are all elder cousins to the School of Science and Arts (already described) in Lower Church Road, and like it were designed by Hans Fowler Price whose office was a short distance west at 28 Waterloo Street - still home to a firm of architects until quite recently. In early 2014, the Boulevard lost its Post Office - over the years it had occupied various sites on the street but now looks unlikely to return.

Crossing the Boulevard to its north side, an extended gabled terrace runs down to the junction with Victoria Quadrant. For as long as can be remembered, these have always served as both offices and residential flats. No. 23 , alone, has managed to hold on to its walled garden and provides a hint of what this part of the street looked like. But no. 1 (now 'Hadleys') has taken advantage of the wide south-facing pavement and sheltering cherry trees to set up an attractive cafe/restaurant with tables and chairs on the sunny side of the street.

Reaching Victoria Quadrant, the next terrace has a Gothic style and was once the Smyth Pigott (Lord of the Manor) Estate Office. Around 2008, these buildings were fantastically disembowelled and refashioned as an Italian restaurant. The Smyth Pigotts would certainly have taken exception to that! I especially mourn one particular casualty of the development: the white flowering crab apple tree at no. 25 whose fruit fermented on a cidery autumn pavement. Next door stands Tivoli Mansions - a block of flats built in the 1980s with a curious sideways stance to the street.[31]

[31]*This area was occupied by the Summer and Winter Gardens in Victorian times.*
It later became home to the Tivoli Cinema which was bombed during the war.
The Victoria Bowling Club, which nestles behind the new building,
is the lone representative of the old Gardens.

Eastward along the Boulevard

Continuing along the north side to where the Boulevard side-steps right to become Gerard Road, there is a mixture of large detached and semi-detached stone houses (of both pink and grey limestone). A mix of offices and homes, most have kept their front walls and some their gardens. There was a period, between the 1960s and early 2000s, when the north side of the Boulevard, along with Stafford Place, was home to many of the town's medical general practices - five in all. As with the hospital, one by one, most have now relocated some distance from the town centre and contributed to an erosion in the character of Weston's premier street. Stafford Place, running north, is one of the few roads in the town to have held onto its early planting of London planes.

The former Library and Museum

Back at the Victoria Quadrant/Orchard Street intersection, the south side of the Boulevard proceeds eastwards with a former Methodist church (now an estate agent) and a terraced run of late 19th century buildings, many with elaborate barge-boards. The Boulevard now meets Alfred Street with Albert Quadrant proceeding north up the hill. On the north-east corner stands a magnificent Holm oak looking out across the road to the old General Hospital - now converted, with great sensitivity, into spacious apartments.[32]

[32]*The original dispensary/hospital in Alfred Street was built between 1857 and 1865, and gradually enlarged with additional wards. In the 1920s, Henry Butt orchestrated public opinion and achieved the construction of the large Boulevard wing. It is beautifully fashioned and on the facings the hard Carboniferous limestone has been worked like courses of brick. The 1990s redevelopment of the hospital was a defining moment in the architectural history of the town. For years, Weston Civic Society had insisted this group of buildings was too important to be lost. This was emphasised in 1988 when all the Victorian hillside received Conservation Area status. There was considerable confusion over ownership of the hospital site - the Church of England had retained an interest since its original donation of the land. Eventually delay made it possible for the developers Fisher & Deane to buy the site economically and to retain and adapt the most significant buildings.*

Henry Butt House (the old hospital)

Continuing on from the old hospital (now Henry Butt House) you come to another Hans Price contribution: the former Weston Public Library and Museum which opened in 1900. In 2012, North Somerset Council abandoned this fine building through a political sleight of hand - an act of cultural folly. The old library is unusual for Weston in that it is constructed largely of red brick with relieving bands of Bath-stone. The carved arched doorway is watched over by Six Muses - sculpted by Harry Hems. The library and reading rooms originally occupied the ground floor with the town's museum upstairs. In 1975, the museum departed for Burlington Street and the library took over the whole building. The Grade II listed building now awaits a new role in life - crazy, because it was a perfectly good library! Meanwhile, the south side of the Boulevard closes with the 1950s telephone exchange (which replaced a fine run of Victorian houses) - its dull, flat panels of concrete, metal and glass have never been at ease on the Victorian street.

Around the corner in Alfred Street, set back from
the road, is Weston's original hospital and dispensary
(1857) - Hans Price yet again. His design, from
early in his career, has been skilfully recaptured in
the 1990s redevelopment (see previous footnote).
Across the road, the conversion of an old
depository warehouse is not so successful but
does conserve the varying roof line of Alfred
Street. Almost next door, what was once
Christ Church Parish Hall on the corner of
Prospect Place, retains the same door onto
Alfred Street I recall as a child.[33] A few
yards further south in Burlington Street,
Weston Museum occupies the former Gaslight Company
workshops (see Special Page). Directly opposite the museum is a charming group of
houses called Meadow Villas, whose back gardens are separated from the museum by
a hotch potch of garages and hard standing. At one time this area was a small market
garden - would it were still so.

'The Muses,' former Weston Central Library

[33] *I used to have school dinners here and difficulty
with the skin on rice pudding. We would troop,
in convoy, from Christ Church School waving to
patients smoking their cigarettes on the hospital
balconies. The school dentist also pulled out two
of my teeth in a room on the first floor - even
though I had a letter saying he mustn't. These
things stay with you.*

The courtyard, Weston Museum

Weston Museum

Weston Museum started life sharing Hans Price's red brick building in the Boulevard with the Public Library - the museum occupied the upper floors. In 1975, the local council converted the handsome, former Weston Gaslight Company buildings in Burlington Street into a new museum. It was an outstanding conversion which opened up the central glass-roofed courtyard floored with its quietening wooden cobbles. The main entrance leads through the museum's shop (well stocked with local books and souvenirs) into the bright courtyard from which the displays and exhibition areas can be reached. These galleries exhibit the geology, archaeology and wildlife of the district - for example; you'll find the Becket Reliquary from Woodspring Priory here.

The courtyard has an evocative collection of enamel advertising and shop signs. There's an Edwardian chemist shop and stories of Weston's seaside. Some of the automata from the old Grand Pier are here; just as Laurie Lee describes them in 'Cider with Rosie' and perhaps even more spooky. Next door to the main building is a small terrace house - 'Clara's Cottage' - furnished in the style of the late 1800s and telling

the story of the people who once lived there. It's a captivating place.

In 2011, North Somerset Council moved to close the museum and sell the buildings. A fierce local campaign encouraged Weston Town Council to take on running the museum although with much reduced curatorial support. Clara's Cottage was also saved although other buildings were lost. The museum has now won a Heritage Lottery Award of £1.2 million for a complete refurbishment - its future now looks very bright indeed!

Alfred Street carries on south, past the Meadow Street/Baker Street intersection, with terraces of two and three storey town houses opening directly onto the pavement. It has lost most of its shops. Meadow Street, like the High Street it eventually joins, is a vestige of the old village and follows a meandering way. As the village grew into a town, Meadow Lane (as it then was) lost its orchards and fields which gave way to workshops, pubs and shops serving the young community's working families. With Baker Street, Orchard Street and Orchard Place, it remains a marvellous assortment of businesses and is one of Weston's great assets - even though its many butchers and wet fish shop are long gone. It's here you get your keys cut and trousers altered, guitar strings, a ukulele, walking gear from 'Outdoors & Active', army surplus, a tattoo or two, barbers and hairdressers, bird seed, Lego, Coles for shoes... In 1942, after it was bombed out of the High Street, Marks & Spencer took up residence in the shop on the west corner of Meadow Street and Orchard Place.

Running north and south from Meadow Street are residential roads Alma, Palmer and Hopkins Streets.[34] Each of these has its own character, partly depending on the materials used in their construction, the width of the street and the vista (or not) it opens on to. Palmer Street is rather classily finished in local stone whereas other streets, which are a bit older, are mostly rendered. Some of the houses have miniscule front gardens and others front doors that open directly onto the street. In Alma Street particularly, houses have been pushed up a social notch or two by the addition of a fine bay window. Baker Street continues east from Meadow Street with Jubilee Road, George Street and Stafford Road running south. The late Victorian villas here are all built of local limestone and mostly semi-detached. They are lovely houses, but sadly, many have sacrificed their small front gardens and gate pillars for parking; bringing about a rather broken appearance to the streets.

[34] *It is difficult to believe that the 1960's Town Plan demarcated the Palmer Street area for demolition in order to build a central car park! Planning blight undermined a thriving community with many houses being sold to the council at depressed prices and families moved to outlying estates with great sadness. Only when the threat of destruction was lifted did the area return to something like its old self - houses in the heart of town, perfect for older people and those who neither wanted or needed a car. All the same, that doesn't excuse the council's proscriptive parking charges for residents in central Weston - they need to be encouraged to live in town.*

Behind many of these houses are workshops and old stables, usually revealed by narrow lanes and arched passageways. Above the archways sit an additional room or two - little space is wasted. Tucked away behind these terraces are forgotten cottages - keepsakes of the old village. Surrounded by the advancing streets they became lost from view, and here they remain hidden, forsaken memories, forgotten lives. In Cross Street (which runs between Orchard Street and Alma Street) stands a three storey, former corn chandler's business which, until 2001, retained its high loading door and sash windows - now rendered anonymous by infilling and uPVC. There are other back ways between these old streets with hidden entrances and exits, where the traces of an older Weston can still be found.

Chapter Eight

THE TOWN - PART 3

The Odeon Cinema

To the south, Alfred, Alma and Orchard Streets open out onto the trees and raised lawns of Alexandra Parade. This area has changed much over the past 30 years or so - mainly through the construction of the large Tesco store (with apartments on its upper two storeys) on old railway land. The railway had arrived in 1841, but because genteel Weston didn't want dirty steam trains in its midst, the Bristol and Exeter Railway Company had to swing the line across moorland with a small junction station a few miles south-east of the town. A branch line, served by horse drawn carriages, then transferred passengers to the town centre pulling up just where the Floral Clock now stands - with a pub close by (now forever changing its name) originally called the Railway Inn.[35]

[35]*In 2006, blacksmith Nathan Bennett modelled a scaled replica of the mid-19th century Robert Stephenson locomotive 'North Star' (in memory of Axentis Michael); to mark the site of Weston's first railway terminus and celebrate the 200 years since the birth of Isambard Kingdom Brunel.*

Eventually a loop line arrived (1884) and what had become the Great Western Railway built a fine station about a quarter mile east of the town centre. The area previously occupied by the railway became known as Old Railway Square and was planted out with trees and lawns. Later it was called 'The Plantation' - a name still used by many who have lived in the town all their

Weighbridge kiosk, Alexandra Parade

lives. Incorporated in this landscaping was a weigh-bridge with an Arts and Crafts, half-timbered kiosk - still standing but sans platform - stranded on a small island at the eastern end of the Parade. In 1935, the Floral Clock arrived; its flower bedecked hands and cuckoo captivated visitors for many years until they eventually succumbed to vandalism and cuckooed no more.

Traffic schemes have succeeded in converting this open space into something of a race track - you cross it in fear of your life! The Civic Society planted horse chestnut trees around the circumference of the central lawns and rescued the original Plantation streetscape to some extent, but high speed traffic still needs to be curtailed.

Tesco cosies up against the Odeon Cinema whose flat Deco tower of pale buff tiles dominates the Parade. The Odeon, designed by Thomas Cecil Howitt, was part of 'The Centre' shopping development in 1935 which included a glass canopied pavement curving away towards the Town Hall - most of which has now been lost, along with the period shop fronts and metal framed windows. Also lost are the lime trees that once shaded the pavement here.[36]

[36]*Grade II listed, the Odeon had a major restoration a few years ago with many of its black 'Vitrolite' tiles being replaced. It remains a fine building. The main theatre has been divided into two, but the screen sizes have not been sacrificed. In addition, two studio theatres have been cleverly fitted in. The ambience of the stairway to a first floor lounge, complete with languorous settees, remains a distinct cinema experience. A luminous Compton Organ is still there, rising and falling, with lights aglow on special occasions.*

Walliscote Road runs due south from the Odeon for nearly a mile. Magdala Buildings, opposite the cinema, curve around the corner into Alexandra Parade. These shops and offices, designed by Hans Price in 1869, linked a burgeoning High Street with the civic area around the Town Hall - its elegantly fashioned Bath-stone facade of curved gables and windows has worn well. A small cobbled back lane divides Magdala Buildings from a pub which sits on the corner of Oxford Street opposite the Town Hall. Also subject to multiple name changes, this pub was originally called the Bristol and Exeter Hotel; a direct link with the company which brought the railway to Weston.

Oxford Street moves west from The Centre to the sea-front. Along its northern pavement stands Southbourne Terrace and although shops and restaurants have filled the terrace's front gardens, the original houses are still there; peering down from their first and second floors. Other than the former Bristol and Exeter, nothing remains of the Victorian period at street level. Across the road it's quite different with the Town Hall and Emmanuel Church dominating the scene.

Town Hall portico

Building the first Town Hall was surrounded by a swirl of controversy and alleged corruption, but was eventually completed in 1859. In 1897, Hans Price succeeded, brilliantly, in absorbing the earlier hall into the present self-assured public building. It came complete with a new clock-tower (which owes not a little to Big Ben) and a gabled meeting room, above the original main entrance, astride a five-arched portico. It remains a fine building despite the ponderous, brown brick, 1980 and now modified Annex. Part of the earlier Town Hall, which once contained the old Weston Borough Council Chamber, can still be seen in Oxford Street in the small open area next to Emmanuel's churchyard.

In 2010, North Somerset Council (with an almost monopolistic administration) decanted a large number of Town Hall staff into offices the council had bought in Clevedon. This left an all but empty Town Hall, subsequently refilled by the costly evisceration of the Annex to accommodate a 'hub' of local services. This is where the library ended up. The open plan of the 'hub' is a light and pleasant space, but that doesn't justify its cost and Weston's loss of local employment, amenity and heritage. (The town centre had already lost its hospital, followed by its law courts and police station.)[37]

Emmanuel Church, Weston's second church, was built in 1847 and came to be through the extraordinary energies of a young curate attached to the parish church: Rev. John Hamilton Forsyth. Respected for his devotion to the poor (at the time, the area around Emmanuel was very working class), he died just as the construction of his church was being completed. The church tower has some fearsome gargoyles which look out over the town with snarling disapproval - including, at the time of writing, the demolished ruin of Dolphin Square!

[37] When unloved Avon County Council was disbanded in 1996, Woodspring District Council metamorphosed into North Somerset Unitary Authority (Council). After 20 years, Weston was (nearly) back in Somerset again! In order to accommodate the enlarged authority, the Assembly Room of the 1858 Town Hall was furnished as the Council Chamber. The fitting out, using cherry wood and other natural materials, succeeded in rejuvenating what was a lacklustre and underused hall. With the refurbishment, the meeting room above the entrance portico returned to its original Hans Price proportions and beautiful encaustic floor tiles were revealed on the entrance lobby's floors.

Just south of the Town Hall stands Hans Price's finest (for Rosie and me) Weston building - Walliscote School. This was formerly known as the Board School and has gone through any number of primary and secondary educational manifestations. It's made up of a series of high roofed pavilions linked by single floored gabled classrooms. The roof peaks are crowned with elaborate ventilation 'lanterns' and the theme of high and low roofs is repeated in smaller buildings to the rear. There is also a charming, half-timbered, Arts and Crafts outbuilding tucked in around the back.[38] The entire formation, a cascade of roofs, high lanterns and Bath-stone, catches the sun and glows with reflected light. It's an uplifting education in itself.[39]

Walliscote School

Half-timbered outbuilding, Walliscote School

[38]*Rosie recalls this being used by her school in Locking Road (Winterstoke) as an office-cum-storeroom. It has also been used as a classroom and a kiln room. It is now planned to be a kitchen where children can learn to cook.*

[39]*Hans Price's pavilion theme is repeated at what was Wyvern School in Locking Road (formerly a Board/Council School and later called Winterstoke Secondary School for Girls + Ashcombe Primary) saved from destruction by an imaginative conversion into flats. The work was carried out by Fisher and Dean. The same firm which rescued the former General Hospital in the Boulevard.*

Hans Fowler Price - Weston's Architect

As described in the main text, Hans Fowler Price was responsible for much of Weston's finest architecture. What isn't generally realised is that much of the town's domestic buildings also arose on the drawing boards of his office in Waterloo Street.

'Bourn' 7, Trewartha Park

Hans Price was born in 1835 at Langford in Somerset.

He trained as an architect in Liverpool and opened his first office in Weston High Street in 1860. He cannily married Jane Baker whose father, Samuel, was a partner in Lords of the Manor, Smyth Pigotts' firm of solicitors - Price eventually became the consulting architect for the Smyth Pigott Estate. He revealed a flair for detail that would make a straightforward house a little special and maintained this individuality when the opportunity arose for his Grand Works. These he carried off with enormous self-confidence and his buildings are now an inimitable part of the Weston scene. He recruited styles from wherever he fancied. The Mercury Office was apparently inspired by Spain's Cathedral of Saragossa. He gathered the Arts and Crafts movement into his design for the School of Science and Art and medieval Tudor at the Constitutional Club. There is a Germanic influence in the draped facades of Walliscote School.

Price and Jane lived at 'Tyn-y-Coed', 48 Hill Road for 30 years, then at 'Bourn' (named after Jane's family home in Burrington), 59 Boulevard. They finally moved to another 'Bourn' at 7 Trewartha Park. They had four daughters and one son. Hans Price was churchwarden at Christ Church (whose enlargement he designed) and Chairman of the Weston-super-Mare Gas Company. He was a keen chess player and invited various chess champions to play in Weston. The Mercury obituary describes a man with tremendous energy, who remained mentally active to the last. He was still busy in his office only a short while before his death in 1912, aged 77 years. His wife and son predeceased him.

From the Town Hall, Station Road runs eastward to the Railway Station with Tesco's store to the north. On its southern side stand the former Court House (now residing in Worle) and the rather sombre stone of Victoria Methodist Church, although the mood is lightened by the high arched doorways and turret of the Nightingale's depository building next door. As previously described, Tesco's fills what was originally railway land where Weston's second station was built in 1866. It was here that visitors began to arrive in great numbers.

The arrival of the Great Western Railway's loop line in 1884 meant the town, at long last, had main line services requiring a new station - Weston's third. The Victorian station is largely intact, built of local stone, mostly single storied with high chimneys, it embraces both sides of the track - although some of its Great Western character was lost when its glazed canopies were replaced by modern equivalents. Embossed cast-iron columns and fretwork detailing remain along platforms where trains still arrive and depart following the railway lines' satisfying curve. I remember the coal fires burning in the waiting rooms and the blast of steam as locomotives prepared to depart. Steam trains still make special excursion visits to Weston (the Torbay Express) when the evocative sound of their steam whistle can be heard across the town. Over the road from the station stands an engaging group of 1930s flat-roofed houses - they still look challengingly modern and must have appeared revolutionary in their day. It's a shame so many of the horizontal iron-frame windows have lost out to the ubiquitous uPVC.

On the southern side of the station stretches an area of sports playing fields (the Recreation Grounds) known locally as 'the Rec', alongside Weston Rugby Football Club which has occupied its land here since 1880.[40] For some time this part of town was not entirely healthful for across the road stood the Gas & Coke Works discharging its noxious pong of bad eggs and sulphur! Its high gas holders were dismantled in 2014 - the coke works were long gone.

Back at the Town Hall and moving south past Walliscote School, we enter a part of the town where grand houses generally preside. Some have towers and turrets with bay windows which provide a panoramic view of the street. The large windows allowed more light into rooms which the Victorians, perversely, cancelled out with drapes and heavy curtains to protect their furnishings from the sun! At least the sombre colours gave the servants an easier time by disguising the soot and the coal dust. Wilton Gardens, a small square chopped off by Walliscote Road, has rather smaller detached and semi-detached villas (with names like Pembroke and Woodville) arranged around a walled garden. Most of the houses are built from the local light-grey limestone but along its north side there is a yellow brick terrace which would be more at home in London. A curious translocation. Just beyond Wilton Gardens, at 42 Walliscote Road, is a house called 'Varzin' - the boyhood home of Arthur Stanley Eddington (1882 - 1944), a senior figure in 20th century astrophysics. On the house wall above the pavement, there is a detailed bronze plaque with a relief portrait of the physicist.

[40] *Weston RFC was formed in 1875 following a local newspaper advert by a Dr Julius Wilmot looking to "promote healthy exercise". Following WWI and the subsequent economic depression many Welsh men came to Weston looking for work and boosting the availability of high quality rugby players. For many years the club achieved premier status playing clubs such as Bristol, Bath, Swansea and Cardiff - and winning. Weston rugby has also supplied more than its share of county and international players. It continues as a successful amateur rugby club. (WRFC - 'History')*

Eastern gate to Ellenborough Park with Howard's bike

A short distance further south, Walliscote Road arrives at Ellenborough Park. Although the park was designed primarily to display its fine crescent (described in Chapter 2), it also provided a perfect setting for some serious gentlemen's residences. These encircle the park and where Walliscote Road passes through its northern boundary are two particular examples: to the west, Tower House with its high garret (from where gentlefolk could observe the setting sun or the loiterings in the park below) and to the east, Ellenborough Hall with its coach-house and outbuildings. The coach-house is unusual for Weston where few large houses had their own stables.

South of Ellenborough Park, Walliscote Road intersects with what has been called 'Villadom'. Most of the houses in Clifton, Clevedon and Severn Roads are late Victorian and often they had a dual purpose. They were not just family homes; they also had rooms for paying guests - seasonal visitors to the town. They are substantial houses, mostly semi-detached, two storey with bay windows onto the street. They have small front and rear gardens and a narrow path and wall divides them from the property next door. Although they rarely diverge from the standard, pattern-book, villa formula; the hard, light-grey limestone and Bath-stone detailing give them a strong local identity. The houses crowd all sides of the streets - accompanied by a fine drift of wind-blown sand, the sea sparkling tantalisingly beyond the sea wall to the west.

Villas, Walliscote Road

There was a time here when there were shops on every street corner, as well as one or two tucked in along the street. Most have gone, but Whitecross and Severn Road have managed to hold on to some local businesses - despite the intrusion of a major supermarket convenience store. In Whitecross Road, Iris Hogg's Whitecross Bakery is fighting the good fight with its delicious speciality breads (corn and malty seed loaves especially) and there's Burrough the Butcher's splendid local meat. The houses which became shops, gave up their front gardens to form a wide pavement which extends down

to Severn Road. Until not so long
ago, an extinct grocery store on the
south-east corner of Clevedon and
Whitecross Road still bestowed its
name to this junction. "Brown's
Corner!" would come the bus-
conductor's call. The name of the
original shop, which closed during
the Second World War, can still be
seen (it's disarmingly wonky) in the
doorway mosaic. After a number
of reinventions, including Southside
Video, the shop now supplies
equipment for the disabled.

Brown's Corner

Chapter Nine

THE SOUTH OF THE TOWN

Uphill Castle from the cricket ground

Between the early 1900s and World War II, the area of land south of Clarence Park and west of the railway loop line gradually filled with houses. Moorland Road retained the Victorian villa style but slowly, as in Elmsleigh Road and Broadoak Road for example, more substantial detached houses and bungalows were built with fresh architectural personalities. Westward, since 1892, the land running behind the sand dunes of the Weston Bay seaboard, from the Royal Sanatorium (now Royal Sands) to Slimeridge Farm in Uphill, has been filled by Weston-super-Mare Golf Club. This is a classic links course famously configured in 1922 by Dr Alister Mackenzie.[41] So it's not surprising that local estate agents came to consider this whole area as 'the favoured south ward'!

Up to the 1950s, south Weston came to a halt at the southern boundary of what were then the playing fields of the town's two grammar schools - delineated by the Windwhistle Road. The Boys and Girls Grammar Schools had arrived in 1935, filling the fields south of Broadoak Road. Built of pale buff reconstituted stone in an arresting Egyptian style, the school and its pharaonic clock tower became a striking landmark for the southern entrance to the town - even though the four clock faces rarely told the right or even the same time! In the early 1970s, the grammar schools transmuted into Broadoak Comprehensive. While this was going on, the school buildings were steadily falling to bits so that in 1999, considered beyond rescue, they were demolished. For a while, the clock tower was the last fragment standing: peculiarly perched on stalk-like legs at the end of the school drive. And then came the denouement: my old school being ground up into enormous heaps of hard-core - you don't expect that! These days, it's a disappointment the new Broadoak School is such an ungainly collection of buildings - but they will probably last longer than that handsome, though apparently flawed, 1930s structure.[42]

[41]*Dr A. Mackenzie: Yorkshire born Scot, master golf course designer,*
responsible for the Royal St George in Great Britain and the Augusta National,
home of the Masters championship in the USA - amongst many others.

[42]*The Boys and Girls Grammar Schools, originally called 'The County School',*
moved in 1935 from ex-army huts in Nithsdale Road to a set of magnificent new buildings
in Broadoak Road. Girls and boys were now divided into separate institutions on the same site -
the schools were mirror images of each other with their own quadrangles,
classes and gymnasia but sharing a dividable hall and an imposing clock tower.
Apparently, the tower was chosen in preference to a swimming pool - those were the days
Weston had plenty of pools. Sadly, the attractive, reconstituted stone blocks'
steel reinforcement began to corrode almost immediately (the tower required major work in 1939!)
and by the 1990s the school fabric was deemed unsalvageable.
Presciently, around 1960 a group of six-formers put the school
up for sale in the Weston Mercury - along with a fine set of Victorian Masters
and the headmaster's telephone number!

Facing the school across Windwhistle Road is the high stone wall to the grounds of Uphill Castle/Manor (see Uphill section) and the Weston sewage pumping station. Windwhistle Road then curves south (to become the Bridgwater Road) dividing the individual cricket grounds of Weston Cricket Club and Uphill Castle to its north and south respectively. (By the way, there's a secretive view of 'High Gothic' Uphill Castle from its cricket ground.) The road then leaves the main highway and shrinks to become Windwhistle Lane, travelling north-east (with a footbridge over the railway line) to reach the Bournville housing estate. Before reaching Bournville, the lane forms the northern boundary to the Coronation Estate. As its name implies, these are council houses built in the 1950s. Land available here was also taken up by Uphill Comprehensive School which then became Weston's Six Form Centre - later absorbed and extended by the highly successful and inclusive Weston College. Quite a wide area remains as open space (I remember large tented holiday camps here in the late 1940s and early 50s) with a central zone set up for BMX cycling. Given this is a flood-plain, it's not surprising it often becomes inundated in winter.

Following the Housing Act of 1919, Weston started off its public building with an attractive group of council houses at Milton Green - amongst the very first in the whole country. The beginnings of the Bournville Estate, in the town's south-east, arrived in 1927 on land close to the Bournville Road - from which it collected its name.[43]

Building came to halt here at the onset of World War II, but started again soon after with single storey prefabs and Nissen hut shops.[44] The prefabs gave way to council houses and maisonettes during the 1950s and 60s, with further construction in the Oldmixon area and the already mentioned Coronation Estate.

[43]*Bournville Road was named and had houses long before the estate that
bears its name rose from the planner's drawing board.
Although it's almost certain the name is derived from the famous
Cadbury Bournville Village in Birmingham (erected to house the chocolate factory workers);
the name's arrival in Weston appears to have been the fancy of a
Mr Poole who had bought the land around 1905.
('Yer tiz' Bournville Memories 1995).*

Unfortunately, the railway loop and branch lines have had the effect of isolating these estates from the town and from each other - they have always felt encircled. At about the same time, council and private houses were being built around Earlham Grove, between the Milton and Locking Roads. In the early 1960s, the powerful sewage pumping station off Windwhistle Road came into operation making house building on the low lying land to the north and east of Worle possible. Weston was now set for a massive expansion.

Post war Nissen hut pharmacy

[44]My parents, George and Joy Smith, opened their Nissen hut 'Bournville Pharmacy' in Lonsdale Avenue in 1948 where my father prepared his formidable 'Smith's Blackcurrant Linctus' - a remedy which, to my amazement, contained sulphuric acid! Colds didn't stand a chance.

Chapter Ten

THE HILLSIDE

Villa Rosetta

In his 'Tales of Old Weston', Brian Austin describes the year 1835 when the Misses Pank sent their architect from Italy to design a good house in the Italian style. Well, he picked a perfect spot. Halfway up on the southern Worlebury hillside, above and west of the parish church, he built a beautiful Italian mansion with windowed towers, stables and servant quarters, gate lodges, an ice house and a footbridge linking two parts of the main garden. All the primary buildings were constructed from Weston's softer pink limestone and so the house was called 'Villa Rosa'. It's uncertain how long the Misses Pank were in residence - or if they ever arrived. Indeed, the architect may well have come from Bath! Anyway, by 1847 the formidable Sophia Rooke had moved in.

After the Villa Rosa, large houses sprang up along the hill. They were set back in high terraced gardens and built, largely, with stone quarried from where the houses were going to stand. The hillside became the most favoured area. It was warm and sheltered. Set magisterially above the town, it enjoyed the panoramic sweep of the bay and all the sunshine an English summer might provide.

Villa Rosa footbridge, Shrubbery Road

'Lady' Rooke promoted the development of her Shrubbery Estate and, following her example, similar exclusive enclaves arose on other parts of the hill. They were given high sounding names like Montpelier, Landemann Circus and Eastfield Park and these prestigious groups of houses were often organised around a garden-park or a church. Some exacted a toll for the use of their private roads secured by gatehouses - especially so in 'The Shrubbery'. Sophia sank a well and built a castellated water-tower which supplied the estate. The tower still stands in Shrubbery Avenue and is built with that distinctive Villa Rosa stone. Crossing the small park the water-tower overlooks, you arrive at the top of Shrubbery Road which dips steeply between high stone walls with glimpses of the sea below. The balustraded arch of the Villa Rosa Bridge spans the road just here, but the Italian mansion is missing. The demolition of the Villa Rosa was an act of deceit and duplicity, the worst of many acts of crass, exploitative development that took place in Weston during the 1970s and 80s. The high rise blocks which have appropriated its name are an unfortunate legacy, but a remnant of the old place does still survive. Peeking out over the fence, at the back of the 20th century apartments, is the octagonal tower of the Villa Rosetta. The tower belongs to what was the coach-house and stables of the Villa Rosa and, along with the footbridge, they all carry the signature pink limestone of the lost house. As already described, the stone bridge linked two parts of the garden estate and Sophia Rooke's domain is remembered in the name 'Rosemary' given to the attractive 1920s bungalow built in the eastern garden. A charming closing reminder of the grand house is its sole surviving gate-house, Shrubbery Lodge, pinched in at the bottom of Shrubbery Road. With its oriel and arched windows, gables, high chimneys and a doorway helpfully dated 1839; it's one of Weston's few examples of the Tudor Gothic Revival style!

A short distance to the west of the Shrubbery, the hillside is marked by the high spire of Holy Trinity Church in wide Atlantic Road. Flanked to east and west by two rows of five storey terraces, the church is testament to the enormous self confidence of the growing town in the 1850s. The houses' south-facing drawing-rooms command quite breathtaking views across Weston Bay - and, with a generous dose of beneficial ozone, were the very place to spend summer, far away from the stink and grime of Victorian cities. Long front gardens (some now sacrificed to the car) and the fall of the land emphasise a feeling of spaciousness. Take a look at the three houses at the eastern end of

Shrubbery Lodge

Atlantic Terrace (formerly the Highbury Methodist Holiday Home - now converted to apartments), where the front gardens, walls and gate pillars are all beautifully intact.[45] The likes of St. Neots and Church Mansions began life as large semi-detached houses set in generous gardens on the south side of Atlantic Road below the church. In the 1920s, they were converted, with great ingenuity, into mansion flats using matching stone and windows. It's something of a puzzle to sort out quite where the changes have taken place and where the original houses begin and end.[46]

[45]*A Visitors' Handbook to Weston, dated around 1877, describes the Atlantic Terraces as "monstrous"! - but with "charming peeps up to Worlebury at either end of the church".*

[46]*The mansion flat conversions found in much of Victorian Weston are another of Henry Butt's accomplishments. The wealthy quarry owner realised that, following World War I, Weston's middle class had lost its servants and the means of maintaining large houses. Gentility was preserved however; Butt contrived his apartments to have at least one spacious room.*

Lower down the hillside in Atlantic Road South, the houses are rather smaller, some have resisted conversion into flats and have held on to their conservatories and gardens. There are even a couple of stone bungalows; one named after the northern Italian town of Baveno - something that has always intrigued me!

Prince Consort Gardens, a terraced park at the western tip of Worlebury Hill, looks out to sea above Birnbeck Pier. Once known as 'Flagstaff Hill', this is one of Weston's special places with the whole sweep of the Severn Sea laid out before you: the Quantock Hills and Exmoor to the south; across the estuary to Barry, Penarth and Cardiff (where the Millennium Stadium is just visible); the Severn's mouth with the two Severn Bridges; then back home to Sand Point. And in between: Brean Down to the south, the islands Steep Holm and Flat Holm, and immediately below: the splayed, wrecked elegance of Birnbeck Pier and the bright red doors of its old Lifeboat House.

What's missing, since 2010, is the classical facade of the Royal Pier Hotel (already described in Chapter 1), now a heap of rubble above Anchor Head. Standing well back along Kewstoke Road (which forms the hillside boundary of the Gardens) is a curve of immaculate High Victorian villas. These have recently been splendidly refurbished and restored as apartments but from 1963 they served as the Arts Department of Weston College, and before that as Westcliff, a private boarding school for girls.[47] Above them, peering from amongst the trees, in splendid isolation, is Worlebury Lodge commanding extraordinary views of the Channel. The lodge began life as a Victorian coastguard cottage.

[47] The school, founded in 1899 by the Misses Emily Scott and Marian Gertrude Aldwinckle, started off in Glenfall - a house in South Road, before soon moving to Westcliff; a house on Flagstaff Hill overlooking Prince Consort Gardens and the sea - the central building of five the school went on to acquire. Westcliff survived the tribulations of two world wars - during WW2 most of the boarding girls decamped to Wales and part of the school was requisitioned by the military. Reunited in 1945 (with Miss Aldwinckle still in charge until 1946!), Westcliff continued until 1963 (with well over 200 pupils) when the Church Society in London made the decision to close the school for, it seems, economic reasons.

The Gardens are simply laid out with lawns and flowers. Unfortunately, the flagstaff which once gave its name to the hillside (still in use within recent memory) no longer stands and the small circular pond has lost its ornamental fountain.[48] But the secret boating pool is still there - hiding behind the rockery. On a lower terrace, overlooking Birnbeck, is a fine shelter from where the estuary always puts on a great show; gigantic container ships that can dwarf the islands; the changing textures of the ebb and rising tides; the racing water beneath the pier causeway. Sometimes the air has a clarity that makes Wales seem an arm's length away, the Holms picked out in sunlight. At others, the Channel is cloaked and mysterious - the pier disappears behind a veil, its causeway vanishes into the imagination. On a summer's evening the whole place can become incandescent as the setting sun slides into Wales and the sky becomes a furnace.

The Westcliff Villas

South Road undulates gently along the side of the hill. Enormous houses with sinuous driveways, fronted by pines and evergreen oak, stand high above the road. One (Seafield Court) has a tower standing quite separate from the main building topped by a window-paned belvedere - it had a lift which was used to transport coal to the upper floors of the house (source: Jane Evans).

[48]*A Victorian Visitors' Handbook describes: "a tall flagstaff, gaily adorned with flags on all festive occasions, but in stormy weather carrying one drum, a signal of danger from approaching tempest." In 2013, the gardens came under threat of development; a threat thwarted by the 'Friends of Prince Consort Gardens' succeeding in the Gardens acquiring the status of a 'Town Green', securing their existence in perpetuity.*

The Mediterranean Walls of Weston

Limestone and forgiving limestone mortar have allowed the town's older walls to become a fascinating repository of plant life, and it's intriguing how the sunny spots have become colonised by various Mediterranean and southern European migrants. In summer, the walls are an astonishing display of purple and blue flowers consisting of two species of Campanula - both with impossible names. In Weston, the more frequently seen is Campanula portenschlagiana, the Dalmatian bellflower, which has bright purple bells. Less common but just as vigorous is Campanula poscharskyana, the Serbian bellflower, which has star-shaped flowers of soft lavender blue. Both these plants come from the mountains of Croatia bordering the Adriatic Sea. The Dalmatian bellflower is especially free-flowering, covering walls with a cascade of colour. This hard working plant can often be found in full bloom on even the darkest December day.

A particularly energetic Mediterranean invader is the Red valerian (Centranthus ruber) whose powerful, woody roots can push walls apart. It colonises the cracks and tops of walls with decorative mops of small, scented flowers beloved by butterflies and many other insects. In the Weston area, the flowers are mostly pink rather than red - although a bank of plants can go through a colour range from white to vermillion. The leaves have a bitter taste - I'm told!

The Ivy-leaved toadflax (Cymbalaria muralis) arrived from the Mediterranean region around 1640. It has tiny leaves and small, lilac and yellow, snapdragon flowers. It will pour down a sunny wall with stems up to a metre long - or it can gather at the top, forming a crown of its bright flowers. Another lovely south-east European introduction is the Yellow fumitory (Corydalis lutea) with its clusters of small, bright yellow, tubular flowers and beautiful ferny leaves. It's equally at home clinging to gaps in the mortar or growing in showy mounds at the foot of a wall.

Closer to home, in a wall's shady places; cracks and crevices may be filled with exquisite, small, native ferns - rarely more than a few inches across, they form a delicate tracery. The ones most often seen in Weston are: Maidenhair spleenwort (Asplenium trichomanes), Wall rue (Asplenium ruta-muraria) and the Rusty-back fern (Asplenium ceterach). Rosie and I discovered all three of these on a wall close to our back door!

As the road wends its way, there are aerial glimpses of the town - although, for those of us at road level, selfish, obstructive fencing often gets in the way. To the east, a chimneyed roofscape of Victorian villas tumbles down the hill.[49]

At its eastern end, South Road takes an S-bend and comes to a halt at the top of Queens Road - at the entrance to the Town Quarry. It then continues along the hillside as Cecil Road and on into 1920s Weston. The quarry is a substantial scoop out of the Worlebury hillside (easily seen from the town's promenade) now leased from North Somerset Council by Weston Civic Society and where, nowadays, the Society maintains its headquarters. In the old quarry buildings, the Society has established a cafe, artists' workshops and a blacksmith's forge. Surviving remnants of the quarry machinery have been carefully preserved and restored.

Terracotta boundary marker, Shrubbery Avenue.

THIS WALL
WITH ITS FOOTINGS
IS THE SOLE PROPERTY
OF THE OWNER OF THE LAND
ON THE EAST SIDE THERE OF
THE IRON RAILING
IS A 'PARTY' ONE
A.D. 1899.

[49]*This part of South Road once overlooked the buildings and playing fields of St. Peter's School - attended by author Roald Dahl and actor/satirist John Cleese. Dahl vividly describes his pre-war (not altogether jolly) school days in his autobiography 'Boy'. John Cleese was to return, very happily, to teach in the late 1950s. Like Westcliff, St. Peter's educated the children of civil servants and managers who worked in the Colonies during the days of the British Empire. Many of Weston's grand houses became private schools: Westcliff on Flagstaff Hill, La Retraite in South Road, Eastern House in Landemann Circus and Hazelhurst Collegiate for Girls at Glentworth Hall - at one time, there were more than 30 such schools in the town. Like the Empire, most faded away after the Second World War.*

Seafield Court tower

The Old Town Quarry

However, by far the greater area of the old quarry has been set aside as a nature reserve, for this is a sheltered place which catches the sun and holds on to its warmth. Peregrine falcons nest on the high cliffs where holm oak and red valerian cling on for dear life. Down below, Speckled Wood and Gatekeeper butterflies patrol the edges of the thickets where the wrens clatter. There's often a bunch of squawking crows lugging about the cliff tops. The stone of Victorian Weston came from here - the main source of the stone town. The rock face presents an extravagant palette of colours: red and yellow ochre, muddy conglomerates and light greys. The pink limestone of the Villa Rosa is here. The town is blessed with its beautiful stone and it needs to be treasured.[50] (See Special Page)

Redundant industrial buildings sit low down in the excavated quarry bottom now furnished with meadow grass. This is where limestone was pulverised - in later life most of the extracted stone was used for surfacing roads. On the upper level, the building has been adapted into the splendid blacksmith's forge worked by Nathan Bennett. The quarry's so peaceful now it's hard to imagine its former dust and danger.

[50] *Time was, genteel Weston felt a little too close to the quarry for comfort. During the late 1800s, residents complained bitterly about the noise and dust - but the quarry was there first and the town needed the stone. Even lumps of flying rock arriving on the morning's breakfast table was not a sufficient objection! I well remember the explosive thumps when I lived in Queens Road in the 1940s - but no rock ever crashed into my puffed wheat.*

The Stone Town

During most of the 19th and early 20th centuries, Weston was built from stone quarried out of Worlebury or Uphill. Weston stone is predominantly Carboniferous limestone: a dense, heavy rock, locally light-grey in colour, which formed in warm seas over 300 million years ago. There is also a softer, pink limestone - as was used in the Villa Rosa - which outcrops along the southern Worlebury hillside and Anchor Head. The hardness of the grey stone makes it difficult to work and masons needed great skill in fashioning it. Despite this, house facades often have this stone dressed into squared blocks giving a building a clean and finished appearance.

A cream coloured oolitic limestone from Bath was brought in to border the corners of houses (quoins) and around windows and doors. Bath-stone is so 'soft' it can be cut with a handsaw and is often carved to provide elaborate decoration. Its softness does make it vulnerable to weathering - repairs should always be with new stone or the correct limestone mix. Bath-stone should never be painted - water and frost will get behind the paint and, trapped, accelerate decay. Other than repointing, Carboniferous limestone rarely needs repair. It's so durable the mason's chisel marks can still be seen after 150 years and the worked surfaces remain sharp and defined.

Most of 19th century Weston is built from its home-grown limestone. It's unique and it surely won't happen again. The stone town needs to be protected - Conservation Areas have helped but require emphatic enforcement. Many of the small houses in roads radiating off Baker Street and Meadow Street for example remain vulnerable despite making such a vital contribution to Weston's character. Changes to windows, roof tiles, garden walls, gate pillars, chimney stacks must also be handled sympathetically for they all give definition to the building and the street. Although many of Weston's older houses followed pattern-book Victorian designs, the high quality of their construction and their wonderful limestone makes them extraordinary.

Queens Road was originally known as Quarry Road (too vulgar!) and it leads down from the quarry to the top of Grove Park - described later in the book. Along with its counterpart Grove Park Road, Queens Road is occupied by attractive stone houses standing back behind spacious front gardens. Close by is All Saints' Church (1901, architect George Bodley) which, despite being denied its bell-tower, is recognised as a fine example of '14th century Gothic revival'. Inside, it feels spacious and light with a boarded wagon roof which has endowed it with resonant acoustics. Musicians love playing and recording here. Many of the big houses on this area of the hill have had the 'mansion-flat conversion' treatment and are fused into elaborate terraces. The terrace in All Saints Road, below the church, is different. It was designed that way and is unique in Weston. The houses step down the steep hill with a pleasing symmetry - it's sad the rhythm has been disrupted by two of them sacrificing their stone walls and gardens for car parking.

Bristol Road Lower (or Lower Bristol Road!) runs from the bottom of Grove Park for a mile or so, west/east, along the side of the hill to the top of Ashcombe Park.[51] Running from it, roads like Southside, Landemann Circus, Eastfield Park and Montpelier all aspired to the grand house style of South Road. In Lower Bristol Road itself, many of the houses have a more domestic scale and have resisted conversion into flats. Further down the hill, especially in Albert Quadrant and Southside, a good number of the houses are built from the soft pink Weston limestone - probably quarried in the immediate locality. A particularly striking example of this is Bristol Road Baptist Church (1871) which, unlike its young rival All Saints, manages to come complete with an open octagonal belltower and marble pillars!

Montpelier rises steeply with the spire of Christ Church (1855) looking out over the town. Opposite the church, Christ Church Path steps back down the hill, between walled gardens, the short distance to Christ Church School - which both I and author Jeffrey Archer attended! Further up, another set of steps (Montpelier Path) descends to tree-lined Stafford Place and provides an unobstructed view of this part of the hillside. There is still a wide tract of sloping land running, like a combe, up through the gardens of west Montpelier to the water reservoir opposite Eastfield Park on the Lower Bristol Road. Looking from the back gardens on the east side of

Stafford Place; trees, stone walls, the high gables of St Owens (now Kairos) and Chelford Lodge culminate with the Christ Church steeple and its gold weathercock catching the sun - a perfect setting. In summer, the sky can be filled with swifts swirling and squealing above the hillside - or flying in demented squadrons low along the Boulevard at impossible speeds.

Christ Church Path

[51]*The Upper and Lower Bristol Roads follow the old route from Worle into Weston, tracking along the high ground and avoiding the flood-vulnerable plain below.*

Ashcombe Cemetery

The Victorian hillside effectively ends at Ashcombe Cemetery (see Special Page); its wonderful open setting was inspired by the 19th century Garden Cemetery movement. There are some large houses here which back onto the woods along Lower Bristol Road, and up to Manor Road there's a mixture of 1920 and 1930s developments built on land of the now disappeared Manor Farm. Until 1970, Manor Road marked the western boundary of the Lodge Estate, and up until that time cows still grazed the slopes that fell away from the Lower Bristol Road. The Lodge itself was hidden behind trees on the north side of the road (quite a few of those trees still survive, along with the estate's stone boundary wall), the house and its terraced gardens merging into the woods. Sadly, the fine main building was demolished in 1977 and, like the Villa Rosa, only its stables and coach-house survive - along with its West and East Lodges (gatehouse bungalows) on the Lower Bristol Road.[52]

[52]*The Lodge was built for the 8th Earl of Cavan in 1863.*
It was later purchased by John Jeremiah Jackson-Brown who lived there
with his wife, son and six daughters. He died in 1940 aged 96.
His son was killed in the First World War, only one daughter married
and none had children. The entire family was devoted to public service.
The last daughter, Enid, died in 2000.
At that time she lived at the Old Rectory in Christon
where the sisters had moved when the The Lodge was sold in the early 1970s.

Chapter Eleven

WORLEBURY AND THE WOODS

Entrance to the woods at Eastcombe Road

Along the south side of Worlebury Hill, from Birnbeck to Wood Lane at the top
of Manor Road, there are around eight pathways up into the woods. Some involve a
flight of steps: such as from Camp Road, or alongside the Town Quarry or at the top
of Arundell Road. Other ways just meander into the trees, as in Eastcombe Road and
Wood Lane - although all end in a fairly steep climb to reach the crown of the hill.
Many of the early houses, whose gardens back on to the woods, had private gateways
through a rear stone wall. That wall (some of it still standing) was built around 1812
when the Lord of the Manor, John Pigott, enclosed the land in Weston-super-Mare.
Villagers' sheep and cattle were forced from their traditional grazing land while Pigott
proceeded to develop his private 'game-preserve'.

Nowadays, 'the Woods' are so much part of Weston's setting it's difficult to imagine the town without them, but you only have to look across to Worlebury's sister promontories: Sand Point and Brean Down, to get a picture of how things once were. There, a grassy downland is maintained by grazing rabbits, sheep and cattle. Worlebury became wooded at the instigation of the Pigott family and was essentially enclosed woodland until the end of the 19th century.[53] Eventually, open access was granted to the town and its visitors.

When the woods came up for sale in 1936 at a price of £10,000, Weston Borough Council, astonishingly, elected to decline the offer. The Second World War came and went and the development potential of Worlebury Hill was then soon recognised. Eventually, the Council performed an about turn and stumped up £22,500 and for less land! If the war hadn't intervened, there's a real chance little of the woods would have been left.[54] In the end, the town acquired over 300 acres, stretching from Birnbeck to Worlebury Park, taking in much of the southern slopes above the Victorian building-line and all the steeper northern side right down to the hill's rocky Sand Bay coastline. Since then, Westonians have been able to continue enjoying the woods as they had done since the late 1800s.

[53]It seems, Lord of the Manor, John Hugh Smyth-Pigott, got the idea of a wooded estate following a visit to Sir Walter Scott in Scotland - returning enthused by the writer's love of trees. The story is that Smyth-Pigott then enlisted local children to plant acorns and seedlings - it took several attempts to get the woods established. By the early 1900s, the trees were mainly conifers with abundant red squirrels in their preferred habitat. During the First World War, the woodland was practically clear-felled. Since then, a rather random assortment of native and non-native trees has become established along with grey squirrels displacing the red.

[54]In the 1950s, I recall advertising boards going up close to the water-tower, erected by a development company offering building land on the northern slopes of the hill. Houses only got as far as Cliff Road in the Worlebury Park area - but it was a near thing.

Only a small proportion of the walkers in the woods get there by the southern hillside paths. Most park their cars on the wide stony road which runs from Worlebury Hill Road to the water-tower, and set off from there - these days accompanied by a surfaced trackway. Prior to the D-Day Landings during the last war, large numbers of American military vehicles were parked here under tree cover.[55]

The water-tower (along with a few telephone masts), surmounting the hill's summit, provides a convenient landmark; it has been standing there since 1924 as a reservoir for the hillside town and nearly all the main woodland paths and bridleways converge beneath it.[56] Two paths that run off to the south-east and south-west arrive at Wood Lane and Arundell Road respectively. The south-east path passes on eastwards through an area known as Ashcombe Wood designated as 'ancient woodland' - ie. in existence since before 1600. When sheep grazed the hill, it was protected by an encircling wall - a remnant of which still stands. This part of the hill has several abandoned quarries hidden amongst the trees - now sealed off behind security fencing. Time was, children were able to explore and fall off these places (I did). The quarry above Wood Lane is occasionally used as a theatrical amphitheatre - a splendid oak tree stands guard at its entrance.

Moving west from the water-tower, the stony road (with the surfaced track) proceeds along the crest of the hill. After about 200 metres, it passes, on the right, a curious low pile of stones or cairn called Peak Winna - now difficult to find amongst the trees (This might help - GPS: 51° 21' 18" N 2° 56' 37" W).[57] The road now divides, with the more northerly (once known as the Fishermen's Path) descending to Birnbeck and the Toll Road, while the upper path continues straight ahead to an Iron Age hill-fort or what Westonians once called 'The Ancient British Encampment'. (See Special Page) The track passes through the fort's encircling ditches, its collapsed eastern rampart walls curving away to the south. Unfortunately, tree growth has so cloaked the ten acre site it's difficult now to understand how important this place once was. Not far west of the walls and moving through the camp, land has been cleared of trees to reveal the many Iron Age storage pits - they're up to five feet deep, so look where you're walking! In the clearing, the precipitous northern edge of the hill looks out over Sand Bay while the path continues on to the tip of the Worlebury promontory. Not so long ago, there was a clear view of Steep Holm from here and a seat to enjoy it. The prospect is now lost behind a vigorous growth of ash and holm oak. Steps take you down (I counted 167), past the supremely positioned former coastguard lodge, to Camp Road and St. Joseph's Church.

[55]*Military use continued for some years after WWII - I remember Champ jeeps with Rolls Royce engines being tested along the stony road.*

[56]*The water-tower was once mysteriously enclosed by high stone walls and huge green gates. The main Weston reservoir is at the top of Montpelier. The earliest general water supply for the town was from an energetic spring at Ashcombe - sited at the bottom of Ashcombe Park. That original spring is no longer used and most of Weston's water now comes from the Mendips.*

[57]*Peak Winna (or Picwinner) is a cairn possibly created by fishermen who tossed a stone onto the pile for good fortune. As they passed they called out "Picwinner, Picwinner, pick me a good dinner!" Winna may have been St. Winna, Bishop of Wessex in 660 AD. Dymond describes excavating the cairn in the late 1800s and finding: two bits of bone, three limpet shells, a tobacco pipe, broken bottles, a pin and some charcoal - probably from a picnic fire! After its rediscovery in the 1970s, the council rather spoilt things by augmenting the low cairn with a load of extra stones!*

Worlebury Hill-fort
'The Ancient British Encampment'

The hill-fort occupies the western end of Worlebury Hill. The promontory was probably first fortified during the hostile late Iron Age (post 300 BC) and occupied by the Dobunni tribe whose tribal area extended from the Gloucester region. Any ship's captain sailing the Severn Sea would have regarded the Worlebury hill-fort and its formidable defences. It's a great shame that over the past sixty years, the fort ramparts have been overwhelmed by woodland growth, masking its visual impact and strategic power.

The fort's northern side had the hill's steep protective cliffs, but to the south, east and west massive dry stone walls and deep ditches were constructed. These defended the fort's most vulnerable approaches: from the east - the relatively flat hilltop - and the graduated southern hillside. The especially exposed east had a deep ditch with two enormous defensive walls and a further five ditches. The walls had a complex structure of buttressing and rose to some 10m (30ft) with a base width of about the same.

The main entrance was on the southern flank (which can still be made out) where the walls turn inwards to form a defensible passageway. There were smaller gateways at the north-east corner and in the west - the latter may have provided access to a fresh water spring at Spring Cove - lost following a landslip after the toll road was constructed. There are two further eastern ditches which run in parallel northwards and which probably demarcate a corralled area for sheep and cattle.

Within the ten acre fort enclosure are a large number pits left open since they were first excavated in 1851 and later in 1881. Most of these would have been used for storage - the remains of barley, wheat and oat grains have been discovered. Other pits, which were probably positioned within Iron Age houses, revealed small personal items such as rings and earthenware fragments. The houses themselves were of varying size and built with dry-stone walls and conical thatched roofs - the largest, 15m (50ft) in diameter, was probably the headman's. An area of woodland has been cleared to show some of these features.

It seems that life at the hill-fort came to a tragic end with attack and massacre. The original excavation came upon the remains of about eighteen individuals, ten of whom, both men and women, showed evidence of wounding. One pit contained three bodies and one skull had been "gashed with seven sword cuts". There was evidence of burning on the entrance walls. Spearheads and pikes were found. Just who the enemy was remains a mystery. The Romans didn't usually resort to massacre; they normally took slaves. More likely it was another Iron Age tribe, attacking before the Romans arrived in Britain.

(For a full account see 'Worlebury' by Jane Evans, 1980. Also, a large number of the hill-fort finds are on view at Weston Museum).

North east bridleway, autumn

Back at the water-tower, the north-easterly bridleway, etched into the steep hillside, descends through beech woodland to the Kewstoke end of the Toll Road where a small, castellated gatekeeper/woodsman's lodge once stood.[58] The dense beech canopy suppresses the undergrowth here and you can see a long way between the trees. In autumn, for a week or two, this bridleway becomes a golden corridor of beech and beech saplings, the track traced in yellow and bronze fallen leaves. About 200m down the path, at the base of a large, heavily engraved beech tree, lies an old mounting-block unseen and not much used these days - though horses still pass by. Many big trees, felled during the 1989 hurricane, lie end up - their corpses and root balls decaying on the woodland floor.

[58]*Kewstoke Road - still called "the Toll Road" despite tolls being deemed uneconomic a while ago - follows an old path-line, the Black Rock Path, from Weston to Kewstoke which terminated at the Mulpit Stone in Sand Bay; a boundary marker to the manor of Weston-super-Mare and now lost. The new road was built in 1848 by John Hugh Smyth-Pigott as a scenic extension to his estate. It's a beautiful road, running the northern circumference of the hill with Birnbeck and Sand Bay glittering between the trees and now in danger of becoming over-trafficked. A recently constructed companion footpath (adopting the old 'Black Rock' name) now accompanies the road at a remove a little way up the hillside.*

Where the pathway ends, just above the Toll Road, there's a group of sweet chestnut trees. After a hot summer, plump prickly chestnuts will be scattered about - enough for you and the squirrels. There was a time when this area of the woods was filled with bluebells in spring - they're still there but advancing scrub is making their life difficult.

As already described, the eastward road from the water-tower runs along the crest of the hill. The trees here are a mix of ash, beech, sycamore, wych elm (hiding from Dutch elm disease), holm and Turkey oak, sweet chestnut, field maple, stands of yew, with hazel and holly in the understorey.[59] It's a higgledy-piggledy assortment which underlines the wood's rather random planting. Beech trees predominate where the hill dips towards Sand Bay. About midway along the top road, an adventure playground has been erected where children can learn to climb - without falling off the sides of abandoned quarries! Meanwhile, down the woods' eastern edge, alongside the gardens of Cliff Road where bramble and scrub haven't managed to get a hold, in late April and May, bluebells abound in the numbers I remember as a child.

[59]*While I'm writing this, the ash, a dominant native species in the woods, is under considerable threat from the disease 'ash die back' caused by the Chalara fraxinae fungus which arrived in Britain in early 2012. Parts of continental Europe have lost nearly all their native ash trees. It's hard to imagine Weston Woods without its feathery ash-leaf canopy.*

The upper entrance to the Smyth-Pigott wooded estate was marked by a woodman's gate lodge which, unlike its lamented Kewstoke sibling, still guards its section of the woods - just east of Worlebury Park Road. Much extended, it retains its quirky castellations and toll house character. For many years, it served the Worlebury community as The Old Lodge Cafe, General Stores and Post Office and came with a cracked, concrete tennis court - which succeeded in defeating me and most of my friends trying to play tennis. On both sides of the hill here, there's evidence of prehistoric field systems and mining for zinc and lead.[60] In relatively recent times, the land between the Old Lodge and Worlebury Golf Course (now occupied by houses) was taken up by market gardens.[61] I especially recall E.J.Wells' strawberry beds on Milton Hill.

The Old Lodge, Worlebury

[60] *This lumpy land of old mine workings is locally known as 'gruffy ground'. Many areas of Worlebury have been similarly worked. German miners first arrived here in 1566, but it's likely the Romans were in on the act long before. Mining for zinc was still going on in 1829 and lead as late as 1845. Yellow ochre (iron hydroxide) was still being taken from the south slopes in the 1920s.*

[61] *Much of Worlebury's sunny slopes, from Milton into Worle, was filled with market gardens, big and small. They supplied Weston with its vegetables, fruit and flowers for over a century - right up to the 1960s. See 'The Good Earth' by Gillian Moore.*

Footpaths still trace the outlines of those missing market gardens. In Woodspring Avenue, one of the last pieces of undeveloped land has been filled by St. Paul's School, which moved from its Victorian building at the top of Milton Hill in 2002. I remember it full of cauliflowers, potatoes and wild horseradish - the field that is, not the school! Directly opposite the school-gates are Monks Steps which lead down a wooded ravine to the lower part of Monks Hill. The way then descends a stepped wall, passing on down through woodland to emerge opposite St. Paul's Church in Kewstoke. Monks Hill is one of the steepest in the district with a gradient of 1:4.[62]

The Observatory on Worlebury Hill

[62]*It's likely Monks' Steps served as a medieval church-path from Milton hamlet to its parish church in Kewstoke. It was once known as 'The Pass of St. Kew' - St. Kew, a female hermit of local legend, lived in a rocky cell towards the top of the ravine. Monks' Steps are now in the care of the National Trust. Monks' Hill has always been a cycling challenge - I once pedalled to the top without stopping and bent my drop handlebars. (See our book: 'North Somerset Coast in watercolours'.)*

Worlebury Golf Course, which inhabits much of the eastern hilltop, is overlooked by a parade of 1930s houses along Worlebury Hill Road -which delineates its southern boundary. Eventually the houses give way to fields, woods and fairways on either side, with glimpses of the Bristol Channel and open views to the Mendip Hills.[63] I once came upon a glow-worm on a stone wall along here. After threequarters of a mile, the road ends dramatically at a prominent Weston landmark: The Observatory on Worlebury Hill. This white tower stands like a giant chess-piece at the eastern limit of the hill - at one time the first thing you noticed when approaching Weston by train from the east.[63] Beyond here, the tarmac road peters out as a rough track down into Worle.

A footpath around the Observatory looks out over Worle Quarry, and the view across North Worle and Wick St. Lawrence reveals the relentless growth of the town - Weston appears stalled upon a bluff, poised to pour forward into cowering Kewstoke, Sand Bay and now Hutton Moor. By way of relief, try returning along the tree-lined footpath that threads its way westwards between easeful fairways and greens.

[63] *The Worlebury golf course was founded in 1908 by Henry Butt and his pals for their private recreation. Designed by Harry Vardon (seven times golf major champion) and his brother Alfred. "Not a long course by modern standards (5,843 yards) but with some very tight holes."*

The Observatory began life as a wooden windmill in 1705, to be rebuilt in stone sixty years later following a fire. In 1889 the mill tower was converted into an observatory and tea-room. During World War II, it was used by the Worle Home Guard as its picket post - tragically, one of its number, Jack Crocker Raines, was fatally wounded in a firearm accident. Since then, the tower has lost its lookout cupola and is now part of a private house. It is listed Grade II by English Heritage. These days, trees obscure the landmark view of the tower from the south. (See 'Worle's Windmill' by Raye Green.)

Chapter Twelve

THE PARKS

Grove Park

Weston-super-Mare's early builders had a clear idea about where they were investing their time and money. It was to be an escape from the sweat and toil of the new industrial cities. Weston would be beneficial and health-giving, with ozone galore! That meant, as well as the wide seashore, the new residents and visitors would expect sheltered parks and shrubberies for rest and recuperation.

Many of the private estates included an area of parkland and many of these still exist. Some are in want of care and attention but many, like Eastfield Park for example, are beautifully maintained. In 1856, one of the largest open spaces acquired for the town was Ashcombe Cemetery; from the start conceived as a landscaped garden. During the 1870 - 80s the economy stalled and a beneficial consequence was that land was released by developers and taken up by the town. In this way Prince Consort Gardens (described in 'The Hillside' chapter) and Grove Park became public open spaces, while a donation of land brought about Clarence Park. The land for Ashcombe Park was steadily accumulated over some fifty years before it was formally opened in 1902.

GROVE PARK

In as much as it was Lords of the Manor, the Smyth-Pigotts' pleasure grounds, 'The Grove' really was Weston's first designed open space. Grove House started out as a cottage by the sea and was gradually enlarged during the 19th century. The land around the house was shaped with terraces, shrubs and picturesque walks. In the upper park, J.H. Smyth-Pigott built a stone observatory tower and small quarries were turned into ponds and waterfalls.[64]

[64]*I remember the tower. It was still standing when I roamed the park in the 1940s.*
It stood a few metres to the right of the park entrance at the top of Grove Lane.
It was about seven metres high, built of stone, with steps spiralling up the outside to reach
a circular railed platform at the top - whose centre was missing. Looking down from the top,
the base of the tower was full of branches, rubbish and leaves.
It was a magnet for children and, inevitably, one of us fell off and broke an arm.
So the poor old observatory was blamed and pulled down.

After the Smyth-Pigotts had handed The Grove over to the town in 1891, it was carefully landscaped and a wonderful, ten-sided, cast-iron bandstand (made by Hills Brothers at their Sun Foundry in Alloa) erected on the lower lawn.[65] Since then, the park's topography has, essentially, remained unchanged with the upper ('the top') and lower ('the bottom') areas having distinct personalities. The lower is rather formal; manicured lawns, flower beds, bandstand, the circular pond and the war memorial giving it a precise shape. But as you ascend the various steps to the 'top of the park' the tree canopy thickens, it feels enclosed and dark. This used to be an exciting and wild place where children roamed free - to a park-keeper's despair. It's tidier now and there's a children's playground close to where the old observatory used to stand. An Arts and Crafts shelter is still there. Descending into a wooded vale along the western boundary, there are boulder rockeries, and pools where I used to catch newt tadpoles.

At the 'bottom of the park', the south-facing Victorian shelter has been restyled as a cafe and is a pleasant place for breakfast, lunch or afternoon tea. On summer weekends, there may be music in the bandstand - which may not be entirely condusive to a deckchair snooze. The Grove House was bombed in 1942 and what remains is its coach-house with a modern extension - from a high bank to its right, a mulberry tree drops blood-red fruit in late summer. Weston Town Council is at home here. Immediately in front, you can step down into a walled garden which is probably part of the original terracing. The garden is dedicated to Jill Dando and was designed and constructed in an exciting three days by the BBC Ground Force team in July 2001. Look out for the small tile painting of forget-me-nots by Rosie.[66] The small Gothic building at the park's eastern entrance is the former gate-lodge to the Grove - I seem to remember the park-keeper living there.

[65] *Over the years, the Grade II listed, decahedron bandstand deteriorated to the point of collapse. By 2014, the sounding roof had partially given way. Detailed inspection revealed that a total restoration was required and North Somerset Council responded swiftly. The Weston Trust, Weston Civic Society and Weston Town Council made generous donations towards the repair and the entire structure, including its cast-iron columns, was disassembled, renovated and rebuilt.*

[66] *Jill Dando was shot dead on the doorstep of her London home in April 1999. The man found guilty of her murder was later acquitted and the case remains unsolved. Jill was born and educated in Weston and began her career as a journalist on the Weston Mercury. Her charm and sunny personality suited television perfectly and she became a hugely popular BBC television broadcaster. She was always a passionate advocate for her home town.*

In the 1960s, the Weston Council built public toilets slap-bang up against the main south gates, destroying the approach from the High Street. During the 1980s, Weston Civic Society redeemed things somewhat with judicious stone walls, railings and tree planting - which also succeeded in hiding the car-park along with the loos. Until very recently, you could still see iron railings embedded high in an oak tree next to the south-west entrance - they got there by way of bomb blast in 1941. A 2012 storm brought them back to earth and they have now gained sanctuary in Weston Museum. A short distance from this entrance is a pergola passageway of wisteria and laburnum (passing between the Glebe House garden and the park's forsaken tennis courts) whose fragrance can be intoxicating in early summer. It leads to a scented garden for the blind nestling below the parish church.

ASHCOMBE PARK

'A nice cup of tea' — Ashcombe Park Café, summer

Opened in 1902, Ashcombe Park's 36 acres make it the largest of Weston's parks. The land was originally part of Ashcombe Manor Farm, and during the 19th century development was resisted by the Weston Local Board in order to protect the Ashcombe spring - the town's most important water source at that time. By virtue of being laid out on the southern side of a hill, Ashcombe, like Grove Park, has a marvellous sunny and open aspect and a satisfying mix of copses, combes and sunlit slopes. The main entrance is through gates on the Milton Road and close by are some well tended bowling greens with a splendid open pavilion - it began life as a promenade shelter, close to Claremont Crescent. From the main entrance an avenue of lime trees leads to a shady area of the upper park. There's an Arts and Crafts shelter here (kin to the one in Grove Park) and a park-keeper's lodge. Should it ever get to snow, the western part of the park, which runs down alongside Ashcombe Park Road is great for tobogganing - despite some tree trunk hazard![67]

Entering through the north-east gate, you step down into the park escaping the traffic busying along the Upper Bristol Road. There's a cafe here, where you can sit outside its wooden hut with a pot of tea and enjoy the relaxed grassy slopes in summer. Following the path on down, you arrive at three tennis courts - the most sheltered and pleasant in all Weston. There are few public courts surviving in the town and these were once the most popular. Poor care and neglect has led to self-fulfilling underuse and abandonment. (A while ago, the tennis and 'Pitch and Putt' pay-hut was set on fire providing a further excuse for the council to let things go.) From here, the path passes through a grove of horse chestnuts (excellent conkers) to end just above the bowling greens.

[67]*Sam, our son, has always claimed living in Weston left him with a childhood*
"seriously deprived of snow". And it's true, although there's been a bit more since he flew the nest.
My own childhood seems to have been the opposite.
Living on Worlebury, many schooldays were lost and my Dad's Austin 16
was forever getting stuck in snow on Milton Hill - despite his 'Town & Country' tyres.

Sledging in Ashcombe Park

The Town Cemetery

(Ashcombe or Milton Road Cemetery - take your pick!)

With land taken over from Ashcombe Manor Farm, Weston's hillside cemetery was laid out in 1856 'as a beautiful garden'. This was a style influenced by the Garden Cemetery movement - a home for rare plants and trees, as well as the departed. Up to the 1980s, the main entrance from Lower Bristol Road led down to two charming Gothic chapels built in the pink Villa Rosa limestone: one, to the west, Church of England, the other Nonconformist. For some unfathomable reason, the Nonconformist chapel was demolished leaving its sibling to stand alone, a bereaved twin. The upper gates are still watched over by a pretty Gothic lodge.

Needing to accommodate the burgeoning town, the cemetery took on further land; both from Manor Farm and also Ashcombe House, which once stood in its grounds on the lower hillside to the east. The entrance lodge to the present Milton Road gates originally fronted the carriageway to Ashcombe House - it survived until 1985 as Weston's maternity hospital.

Ashcombe Cemetery remains a beautiful garden with many native and exotic trees. Paths dive and weave between the graves in full sight of the Mendip Hills and the sea. Christ Church steeple rises in the middle distance. In spring, there's an abundance of primroses, lesser celandines, daffodils and bluebells, succeeded by scented banks of cow parsley and sweet smelling rose garlic along the western borders. Summer brings bright battalions of ox-eye daisies, lime tree flowers filling the air with a honeyed scent and a thrumming of distracted bees. And later, the hillside slopes are splashed with the blue of field scabious. Ringlet and Meadow Brown butterflies skim the long grass and wild thyme flowers on the lower scarps. Close to the War Memorial Cross lies the grave of Alfred Leete: the artist/cartoonist who designed the famous Kitchener World War I poster "Your Country Needs You", while tucked down in a sheltered combe in the south-west corner is a small military cemetery with headstones to British, German and Polish war dead. It's a consoling place.

CLARENCE PARK

Main gate, Clarence Park

In 1882, Clarence Park arrived by way of a donation of land by Rebecca Davies
in memory of her husband William Henry. The move wasn't entirely altruistic;
it encouraged further building in the southern areas of the town where development
had stalled. Builder William would have approved of that. Rebecca was subsequently
a bit miffed when the town was slow to lay out the park and so, unsportingly, died two
days before the proposed formal opening! The park finally opened in 1890, named,
for uncertain reasons, after Albert, Duke of Clarence.

The park is divided, east and west, by Walliscote Road, each section having its own
character. Clarence Park West was laid out fairly formally to include a Gothic lodge
with a touch of the Arts and Crafts, a pond and a fountain, shrubberies, trees and walks.
To the south, nearly half has now been taken over by three bowling greens. There's an
attractive chalet-cafe at the park's centre and the houses and trees along the western,
seafront boundary protect it from the Weston winds.

The grassy expanse of Clarence Park's eastern section has mostly been reserved for sport, and sheltering amongst the pines beside the Walliscote Road is the old cricket pavilion. Abandoned now, there was a time the pavilion and the park would spring to life each August for the Weston Cricket Festival; a glorious summer week of Somerset cricket, for which in joyful anticipation my son Sam would say;

"Blue skies over Clarence Park Dad!"[68]

The cricket square, once resolutely defended by wooden fencing throughout the year, has now largely surrendered to hockey and football, although the occasional amateur cricket match is still played.

[68] *The Weston-super-Mare County Cricket Festival was a wonderful annual occasion that had taken place in Clarence Park since 1914, only being interrupted by the inconvenience of two world wars. It was one of those fixed times in the year when you might run into old friends. Originally it took in three Somerset County Cricket matches over eleven days, but in later years shrank to one four day match and a Sunday game. Despite intense efforts by local enthusiasts there was scant support from Somerset C.C.C. and so, after 1996, Weston festival cricket died.*

"Ah, Botham, Richards and Garner of long ago..."

Take a look at Rosie Smith's Clarence Park tile panel at the Winter Gardens, which shows Somerset batting against Worcestershire on August 8th 1991. The time is 11.10am, it's a warm sunny morning on the final day and Somerset are 27 for no wicket. Jimmy Cook is facing the bowler Neal Radford with Peter Roebuck backing up at the Town End. I know because I was there.

Chapter Thirteen

KEWSTOKE AND SAND BAY

On the other side of Worlebury Hill lies Weston's secret seaside. Here the hill's wooded slopes reach down to the Sand Bay shoreline, interrupted only by the Kewstoke 'Toll' Road passing unseen beneath the trees. In spring, this hillside is alight with bluebells and unfolding ferns, sunlight streaming through the open canopy of emerging leaves. Coming out of the woods, down the north-easterly bridleway from the water-tower, the path ends at the Kewstoke Toll Road junction. This is where a gatekeeper/woodman's cottage once stood; its site now filled by a modern house with a room floating above its front door. The adjacent castellated, stone building has spent many of its recent years as a restaurant or private dwelling - there are fine views to Sand Point from its terrace. Sadly, the old Shell Shop across the road is no more - and neither are the public toilets! Below

the walled parapet of the Toll Road (although the toll hasn't been collected for some years now), the way to the beach folds back on itself, curving past the grounds of what was the Kewstoke Convalescent Home. Despite being built in the style and scale of a Grand Hotel, its immaculate whiteness manages to remain largely unseen in its sloping estate.[69] Meanwhile, the road continues down to the beach between the woods and grassy verges.

The road along the Sand Bay shoreline runs its entire length tucked below a grassy embankment with occasional sections of sea-wall. The landward side of the embankment, protected from the prevailing wind, is a profusion of flowers. In early May, amongst high grass, are bright yellow charlock and creeping buttercups, along with the purple flowers of clarey and bush vetch. Sand Bay beach struggles to keep itself tidy with more than its fair share of flotsam and jetsam - wind and currents conspire to deposit a disproportionate quantity of Bristol Channel junk along the bay's strandline. Cleanup volunteers have improved things enormously and let's face it - it's great for beachcombing. With wood from the bay, my brothers and I built a sledge, and our father, not to be outdone, a kitchen cupboard. In 1981, a Great Storm showed Sand Bay's flood defences to be dangerously inadequate necessitating something called

Fishing at Middle Hope

'beach renourishment'. In 1983, this involved pumping sand and gravel from the centre of the Bristol Channel to raise the beach by some four metres (13ft). An Army blockhouse sank up to its gun ports and the old sea-wall below the hill simply disappeared. The new beach was mucky to begin with but has now settled down to a pleasing expanse of sand. Below Sand Point, spartina grass (Spartina angelica) has invaded a substantial area of the beach - this vigorous, hybrid cordgrass was originally planted in 1913, a few miles north, at Kingston Seymore to stabilise the shoreline. It arrived in Sand Bay in 1932 and hasn't looked back. Another misguided attempt at biological control.

[69]*Built in 1933 by the Birmingham Hospital Saturday Fund, the building has retained its dramatic Mediterranean character; something which continues inside with high windows and sweeping staircases. It evokes the atmosphere of a Noel Coward play. During WW2, it served as a military hospital. By 2005, the need for the charitable convalescence it provided had fallen away, and the home became the Cygnet Hospital for the care and treatment of psychiatric illness.*

The Sand Point peninsula, rising to a mere 49 metres (162ft), lacks the pomp of Brean Down, but its smaller scale allows it an intimacy its big brother doesn't have. The sea is nearer and the cliffs less forbidding. On the north side of the Point are the three pebbled bays of Middle Hope with St. Thomas's Head close by.[70] In the near distance stands the tower of Woodspring Priory sheltering below the coastal high ground. You can now reach the priory by a footpath behind St. Thomas's Head, or more easily between the open meadows along Collum Lane from Worle. (see Special Page: 'Woodspring Priory')

Middle Hope

Over the coastal rise, the grass is kept close-cropped by rabbits, sheep and cattle, dry stone walls mark the boundaries of old fields with the Bristol Channel laid out before you. In autumn, the blackberries here make good picking.

[70] *In each of the small bays there is evidence of volcanic activity - underwater volcanoes that erupted 340 million years ago leaving pillow basalt and tuff. St. Thomas's Head is occupied by the MoD. See our book 'North Somerset Coast in watercolours' for a fuller description.*

Woodspring Priory

Three of the four knights who murdered Thomas a Becket in 1170 were from the West Country. One, Reginald Fitz Urse, owned Woodspring (at that time called 'Worspring') which through marriage eventually passed to landowner William de Courtenay. In the early 13th century William built a chapel at Worspring dedicated to "the blessed martyr Thomas" and soon after he asked the Bishop of Bath if he could establish an Augustinian priory - "to hasten the salvation" of himself and his family. All of Thomas's assassins had escaped sanction and expressed little contrition, so it's uncertain if the priory was an act of penance.

At its inception Worspring Priory was not well off, but by the 15th century things looked up and many of the buildings we can see today were constructed. These are: the monastic barn, the infirmary and the priory church and tower (Somerset Perpendicular) which replaced the original chapel. For a century or so life was good for the canons but then came the Dissolution of the Monasteries in 1536 when many of the priory buildings were destroyed and the community suppressed.

In 1849, during repairs to the north wall of Kewstoke Church, a small wooden vessel was found in a 46cm (18 inch) carved cavity. The bottom of the cup was stained, possibly with blood, and it's felt the vessel was probably a 'Becket Reliquary' hidden at the time of the Dissolution. The priory seal actually shows the head of St. Thomas being attacked with a sword, a chalice on a ledge close at hand.

Over the years the priory was used as a family residence and parts of the remaining buildings knocked down and reused in other structures. At the end of the 17th century the priory was aquired by the Smyth-Pigotts who built the farmhouse. It was around this time 'Worspring' became 'Woodspring' - it is not known why. In the late 1800s, it had a brief career as a golf club before reverting to a family farm once again. In 1968, the priory estate along with Sand Point, Middle Hope and St. Thomas's Head were aquired by the National Trust - care of the priory buildings passing to the Landmark Trust a year later.

Back at the Toll Road junction, the Kewstoke Road continues its journey into the village. The road here has managed to remain pleasingly and inconveniently narrow - stone walls and grass verges conspiring to your being pressed flat by passing cars. Despite that, large houses have squeezed onto the hill-slope fields where horses once grazed and wild flowers grew. Up above, the hillside ('the headlands') was kept clear of scrub by a multitude of rabbits, the grass soft and tufty. A wonderful place which my friends and I had to ourselves.

Where Monks' Steps arrive at Kewstoke and St Paul's Church

A short walk along Kewstoke Road and you arrive at St. Paul's Church, huddled at the bottom of Monks' Hill. The small hall, to the west of the church, once served as the village's poorhouse. I remember it as a Sunday School and in the 1950s the entrance was through a small stone porch in the south wall opening straight onto the road. The former rectory, a fine Georgian residence, sits next to the church on its west side amongst shading trees. It provides excellent 'Bed and Breakfast'.

The church of St. Paul has Norman origins and the beautiful carved doorway is from that time, although it probably had earlier Anglo-Saxon or even Saxon origins. It was enlarged in the 15th century and later substantially rebuilt in Victorian times. It was then a remarkable wooden chalice was discovered in the north wall - see Special Page 'Woodspring Priory'. The well tended churchyard lights up in spring with cherry blossom. Immediately across the road by the church is the footpath which runs up to Monks' Steps on Monks' Hill - described a few pages back in the Worlebury chapter.

Gatehouse, Woodspring Priory, high summer

It's a shame so much of the land between Kewstoke Village and the sea is now filled by caravan parks - along with a well-intentioned but incongruous redbrick, village hall. Perhaps inevitably, Kewstoke's pastoral atmosphere is slipping away along with the solitary ambience of its bay. An older Kewstoke of farmhouses and cottages is still to be found beneath the hill. To the rear of the New Inn, at the top of Crooks Lane, are Victory Cottages built in 1759 when General Wolfe defeated the French in Quebec. The New Inn itself occupies the site of an older pub and the Commodore Hotel on Beach Road absorbed a row of fishermen's cottages. And, most famously, there is Electron House (now renamed the Old Coach-house!) on Kewstoke Road where Mr. J. Dando serviced Electron Batteries between the wars!

Chapter Fourteen

THE VILLAGES

Uphill boatyard and St Nicholas Old Church

Perusing an 1809 Ordnance Survey map, Weston-super-Mare barely registers any more significance than its neighbouring hamlets of Ashcombe and Milton. It does have a small parish church, albeit a trifle neglected, but Weston village looks to Worle for most of its needs - especially its ale. The map shows the main route to Uphill to be along the beach (which it calls Uphill Bay) where the sand is flat and firm - the marshy landward track often becoming impassable. The road to Worle is halfway up and along the Worlebury hillside following the present day line of the Lower and Upper Bristol Roads - again to avoid the low-lying land susceptible to flood.

UPHILL

The easiest way to Uphill from Weston is still along the sands. The small unroofed church of St. Nicholas is poised on its quarried cliff above the River Axe - it's here the Mendip Hills seem to pause awhile, before closing with Brean Down and Steep Holm. The church is visible for miles around, from land and sea, and for centuries served as an important landmark - especially so in the days when the tower was whitewashed. Today, the church is picked out by floodlights to glow by night, a sentinel at the southern end of Weston Bay.

The 18th century poet William Lisle Bowles, who so inspired Samuel T. Coleridge, spent much of his childhood in Uphill. His father was rector from 1769 to 1786 and he describes his arrival in the village in his relaxed and conversational verse (spelling as per Bowles):

> *My father came, the pastor of this church*
> *That crowns the high hill crest above the sea;*
> *When, as the wheels went slow, and the still night*
> *Seemed listening, a low murmer met the ear,*
> *Not of the winds: my mother softly said,*
> *Listen! it is the sea!*   *From the Poem 'Banwell Hill'*

Little of Bowles' Uphill remains - his father's rectory is long gone - but you can still hear the sea! His old church looks out from its hill crest over the Severn Sea and a step back to the east is the stump of a windmill - now a lookout tower.[71] Below the north side of the hill, in Uphill Way, are two inns both there in Bowles' time: The Ship (1713) and The Dolphin (1720): each a reminder of the village's maritime ancestry. Uphill has probably been a port since Roman times although whether Mendip lead ever left from here is disputed.[72] Access to Welsh coal explains why the first local brickyards were here - and there were regular packet-boat services to Wales and to Ireland. The last such boat to call was the 'Democrat' in 1942. (P.Newman)

[71]*By 1840, the old Norman church on the hill had become too small and dilapidated; so St. Nicholas New Church was built close to the centre of the enlarging village. In 1864, Thomas Knyfton paid for repairs to the old St. Nicholas but left the nave unroofed - unwittingly creating a much-loved landmark.*

[72]*Speculation abounds regarding possible routes from the Mendip lead mines at Charterhouse and Shipham. Uphill was certainly the closest possible port; the old ways are there and the sense of it irresistible. Only hard evidence, like a spare lead ingot, is missing!*

Today, the muddy banks of the River Axe have a busy clutter of sailing boats waiting for the next high tide. Alongside the first twists and turns of the river lie Uphill Boatyard and its marina pool hunkering below the old church perched high on its quarried cliff. To the left of the boatyard entrance is the closing Marker Post for the West Mendip Way which wends from Wells to Uphill - although you can always start from here should you want to! The beach road (Links Road) meanders by, passing some far-flung holes of Weston Golf Course and Slimeridge Farm, before ending at a World War II blockhouse and the sand-dunes of the southern end of Weston Bay. The scene is filled by the Brean Down peninsula rising above the mouth of the Axe and Black Rock.

The donkey field, Uphill

Nowadays, the village struggles to maintain its physical independence from Weston - made more vulnerable by the arrival in 1985 of Weston General Hospital at the village's south-east corner. The northern borders are safer with Uphill Manor, the woods owned by the Woodland Trust and Uphill Castle cricket ground securing a green boundary between village and town.[73] Entering the village from the north along Uphill Road, there is still a clear sense of separation with shade cast by high trees, the battlemented wall and Gothic gate-lodge of the Manor and an open pasture affectionately known as 'the donkey field' - although donkeys have been absent for sometime. In spring, this field (also owned by the Woodland Trust) becomes an enchanting meadow of bluebells and cowslips. In February snowdrops abound. Old Church Road curves round the field's southern perimeter and wanders between an assortment of 20th century housing and earlier cottages, to end bridging the Great Uphill Rhyne below Uphill Hill. Between here and the sea are a number of small pre- and post-war estates laced with a scatter of Victorian terraces and Coastguard cottages.

[73]*To most locals Uphill Manor is still called by its original name 'Uphill Castle' - it seems newly married Edith Graves-Knyfton changed the name in 1898 because she didn't want to live in a castle! The house was built in 1805 but on being sold to Thomas Tutton-Knyfton in 1853 was enlarged in the 'High Victorian Gothic'. The Graves-Knyftons were generous benefactors to the village and only recently (mid-1990s) gave up the estate. The present owners have carried out considerable restoration which has included reprinted Augustus Pugin wallpapers. The Manor/Castle is now a guest-house.*

Worle village from Lawrence Hill

It's only a generation or so ago Worle, especially on the hillside, stood clear of Weston. From the Windsor Castle pub at the bottom of Milton Hill, the main road used to curve up through market gardens to Worlebury, while Spring Hill, a narrow country lane with high hedges of hawthorn and woodbine, tipped up and down into Worle village. Today, the top of Spring Hill has become a cul-de-sac, and houses have filled the nursery slopes.[74] The old village returns as we approach St. Martin's Church, from Weston, along Church Road. Here the village school occupies what was originally a Monastic Barn. Although little of the medieval building remains, in its proportions and scale, the spirit of the old barn survives - the buttresses along the pavement on Church Road appear to have belonged to the original north wall and tie in with John Rutter's small etching in his book on north-west Somerset.[75]

[74]*Where the top of Baytree Road meets what was the start of Spring Hill, Baytree Garage has been servicing cars since before WW2. Standing to attention, just inside its doorway, is an ancient pump that once dispensed paraffin.*

[75]*The barn was apparently owned by Woodspring Priory and in 1829 John Rutter described its ruin as being of 'superior masonry'. When the old barn became a school Jonathan Ellwell wrote;*

Where once was heaped the produce of the soil,
The lamp of learning is kept trimmed with oil;
Where vagrant urchins loitering near the door,
Heard sounds suggestive of the threshing floor

Just to the east of St. Martin's, the road narrows and turns as it enters the remains of the old village. The houses and cottages here press up against each other - a mixture of the grand and the previously humble - with the roads making themselves awkward in the way they fold back on each other. The Round House, at the top of Lawrence Road, squeezes into the 90 degree angle of criss-crossing roads with no pavements. At the southern end of Ebdon Road, Magnolia Cottage (a big cottage!) retains the only surviving thatched roof in the village.

Directly opposite the church an old footpath cuts north, through the new houses and bungalows, to the steep,

Baytree Garage paraffin pump

wooded hillside below the Observatory (see Worlebury and the Woods chapter). The woodland, enclosed by stone walls and gloomy with the dense shade of Scots pine and Holm oak, may be a fragment of the original coniferous planting carried out by John Hugh Smyth-Pigott in the 1820s. The path itself (Balaam Walk) is confined by the same stone walls but eventually opens out on to a bridleway. This continues up to the Observatory and along the hill to join a footpath which then journeys down into Kewstoke.

St. Martin's was founded in the early 12th century and underwent a major restoration in 1870. One especially poignant tale about the church is that in 1348, the year of the Black Death, four vicars were appointed to its ministry. As each new priest arrived, so he succumbed to the plague, only to be succeeded by another brave man. Considering their close contact with the sick, they must have known that they would almost certainly die – a story repeated throughout the West Country.

St. Martin's is comfortable in its hillside setting. It sits amongst trees and enjoys a south facing churchyard which steps down into a lower cemetery. This, bafflingly, runs out into a bleak tarmacadam car park. The dowdy, beige-brick health centre then completes the disruption of a becoming vista by disconnecting the village High Street from its church.

Worle's High Street is a congested road which has managed to hold on to a few of its Victorian houses: terraced and otherwise. Primrose House (No.188), is a lonely survivor of the 'three windows up, two windows down and a door in the middle' sort of cottage that once frequented the street. Close to Station Road, you can still see the small conical turret of the departed Moorland/ Imperial Laundry. Its title 'The Maltings'

Old brewery turret – Worle High Street

betrays its first life as a brewery. The Woodspring (formerly the New Inn) survives from days when the High Street was called Lower Street and Weston was just a gleam in the eyes of its early developers Messrs Parsley and Cox.[76] Since the 1960s, building has extended far beyond the historic village to form the substantial settlement of 'North Worle' - now fingering eastwards to St Georges and the M5 motorway, and north towards Wick St Lawrence.

[76]*In his book 'The Somerset Coast' (1909), Charles Harper describes Worle ("Wurle")*
as "a detestable village of vulgar and poverty-stricken shops
and out-at-elbows cottages, a blot on its surroundings."
Which seems a little harsh! John Rutter, eighty years earlier, had waxed lyrical;
"pleasantly situated on the south east declivity of the hill.....it bears a cheerful character
and the dwellings have generally an appearance
of neatness and comfort."

HUTTON

Hutton Church from the west

Along the old Uphill to Banwell road lie a number of hamlets and villages occupying the lower slopes of West Mendip. From west to east, they are: Old Mixon, Hutton, Elborough and Knightcott. Of these, only Hutton has managed to resist assimilation; protected by the Airfield (so far) to the north. However, this flood-plain is now in the process of being developed with houses creeping in from the Locking Moor Road. In Elborough, the demolition of an aircraft engineering works led to an explosion of house building such that it now defies the definition of hamlet. Along with its neighbour Knightcott, it's slowly being absorbed into the outer fringes of Banwell. But that old factory did block the view from the Banwell Road - it's good to have a sight of Crooks Peak again, rising beyond Christon Hill.

Hutton is an ancient village dating from beyond Domesday. The Main Road (The Street to locals), which runs from west to east, has many traditional Somerset farmhouses - though their land and orchards are long gone. Some of these houses go back to the 15th century. A lot of post-war housing has appeared north of Main Road, but the heart of the village is relatively untouched. The gravitational centre of Hutton was always a great horsechestnut tree (now sickly and part felled) which stood opposite the school at the entrance to Church Lane. From here, Main Road continues up and out of the village towards Canada Coombe, while Church Lane describes a semicircular route, south and west, past the Old Rectory, Hutton Court and St. Mary's Church.

St. Mary's was completely rebuilt in the 15th century but a church has been standing here since the 13th century at least. It's another beautiful example of the Somerset Perpendicular style. The Victorians did some damage by removing 'a fine southern porch' when they added the south aisle but the church, surrounded by meadows and woods, retains an indefinable tranquility. Immediately next door to the east stands Hutton Court which has been occupied as far back as the 13th century; although it's likely the present building, with its low tower and hall, was rebuilt at about the same time as the church. In the Court gardens, set back from the house, stands a ruined summer house in a picturesque state of decay while in the garden's west wall a small doorway allows manorial passage to the church. The Court's tower was a defensive structure where the family could retreat if under threat. Even the stairway twists clockwise so the sword arm on the right could be used without exposing the body. Not so good if you're left handed of course!

Above Hutton and to the south-east runs Canada Coombe following a sinuous groove through woods to the top of Hutton Hill and passing through the small Mendip settlements of Lower and Upper Canada.[77] From here paths link up with ancient trackways like Bridewell Lane (which leads on to Banwell Hill) and the rather more recently assembled West Mendip Way which takes you to the villages Christon, Loxton or Bleadon depending on which direction you're headed.[78]

[77] *The name Canada Coombe is something of a mystery. In America 'canada' comes from an Iroquois word for 'settlement' although in Spanish, with a quite different derivation, it means 'a narrow valley or glen'. Inspiration may have come from the unification of Canada in 1897.*

[78] *The West Mendip Way was devised (and way marked with oak posts) by local Rotary Clubs to celebrate Queen Elizabeth's Silver Jubilee in 1977. The Way was opened in 1979. It's a wonderful walk of around 30 miles from Wells to Uphill - Rosie and I prefer walking westwards to the sea. See Andy Eddy's guide 'The West Mendip Way'.*

The Airfield

Weston has been described as "a town with a hole in the middle". The 'hole' is Weston Airfield which was planned and approved by the local council in the early 1930s. In 1936, the Hutton Moor was drained and laid out with an airport terminal and a 14,000 sq.ft hangar. The terminal building had started life as a First World War hospital with a control tower fashioned from a redundant seafront cab shelter! All this was leased to Western Airways who flew DeHavilland aircraft between Weston and Cardiff. Later on they established a service to Bristol, Birmingham and Manchester.

The airport was poised for expansion when the Second World War intervened. Western Airways then became involved with the RAF, who also opened a school of technical training (RAF Locking) close by. In 1939, the airfield was requisitioned by the Government with factories building and repairing aircraft such as the Bristol Beaufighter and Avro Anson on its fringes. Weston had a very busy war.

After 1945, there were (briefly) plans to build the huge Bristol Brabazon at Weston as well as the airfield being considered for development as the premier airport for the South West. For various reasons the runway could not be upgraded and the plans came to naught. In 1948, the Weston-Cardiff run was reinstituted with fares of £1.2s 6d return and a journey time of around eight minutes. Commercial flying faded away in the 1950s (and moved to Lulsgate) but gliding and other leisure flying continued into the 1990s - thus conserving Weston's 'hole'.

Bristol helicopters were built at Oldmixon from the 1950s with the factory being taken over by Westlands in 1961. Westlands' Weston operation, after many alarums and excursions, finally closed in 1987. The Helicopter Museum was established in 1974 by Elfan ap Rees (with his own collection of rotorcraft) and in 1988 moved onto land close to the original terminal buildings. Since then the museum has expanded considerably and is now home to over 80 aircraft. RAF Locking closed in 2000 - its land, and now the airfield itself, has been given over to housing development - Weston's 'hole' will soon be filled to the brim! Meanwhile, the old cab shelter control tower survives, rather uncertainly, on the airport's eastern rim close to the museum.

LOCKING

In 1907, Francis Knight described
Locking as a "beautiful little village" with
a road, overshadowed by tall elms, sloping
gently past its old manor house. The
elms have departed, taken out by Dutch
elm disease, although their clonal cousins
survive, disguised as hedges. The trees are
remembered in the name Elm Tree Road.
Sadly, Locking has not been well served since
the mid-1950s, for much of the building since
then has been poorly planned, lacking shape
or coherence. There is no obvious centre
to the village, and where the setting of St.
Augustine's Church was felt to be especially
lovely; its hilltop position is now obscured
by a clutter of housing. The Locking Moor
Road, widened to accommodate Weston

Lintel figure, St Augustine's Church

airport and RAF Locking (a training school), by-passed the village and separated it from
its outer farms. RAF Locking became a small town in itself and since its closure (1999)
this whole area of the Northmarsh is being surrendered to housing.

Locking Manor, situated at the elbow of Elm Tree Road under a great Holm oak,
probably goes back to the time of Elizabeth I although extensive rebuilding masks the
original house. The huge stones in its driveway are thought to have been brought from
'the top of Mendip' where they may have originally constituted a stone circle.[79]

[79] *Francis Knight describes a Rev. Stiverd Jenkins of Weston-super-Mare hauling bullock-wagons of huge stones from*
upper Mendip and using them to landscape his garden at Locking Manor! There's a tradition a stone circle once
stood high up on Mendip. From the nature of the stones themselves and a process of elimination, Dr. E.K. Tratman
speculated that the most likely source was the Priddy area of Mendip - possibly a stone circle close to the famous
Neolithic Priddy Circles. (E.K.Tratman 1958, University of Bristol Spelaeological Society)

Looking across to Locking from below the village on the Hutton to Banwell road, St. Augustine's Church sits on a low hill above Church Farm amongst sheltering limes. Entering the village from the Hutton side, some of the old atmosphere is recaptured in the tiny combe called The Bury, which ends in a hill-start challenge at the top of the ridge. From the church, gazing back across the meadows to the wooded slopes of Hutton Hill and the Mendips and westward to Uphill's St. Nicholas Old Church and the sea, there's a prospect that can't have changed much from when Francis Knight was writing over a century ago.

From St Augustine churchyard looking to Hutton Hill

EPILOGUE

At Clarence Park

The park's still there,
And the old pavilion under the pines.
Each summer I'd wait for August:
The time of tents, marquees and boundary boards,
The outfield mown and mown again.
The square rolled into service.

Dad came here for years,
Way back before the war,
With tales of Wellard whacking balls
High onto St. Paul's roof.
Then he'd settle back, a deckchair and a fag,
Drifting off in the warmth of the afternoon,
His face flushed by the sun.

And then my brothers came,
Often ignoring the match,
Deep in their own game behind the scoreboard and the stands,
Or at lunch or tea, out on the ground
Where a hundred games raced back and forth,
Tennis balls slogged for miles.

Coming back, some years later,
Once again I'd set that week aside.
And then, when you arrived,
Wondered how it might be for you.

So, on that particular day, after lunch,
With Botham and Richards coming in to bat,
A sunny summer's day,
I scooped you up, crossbarred,
And pedalled to the park in restless anticipation.

They didn't let you down.
The ball smashed into the boundary boards
And soared above the pines.
(At least that's how we remember it)
You were transfixed
And Augusts became geared about that precious week
With Waugh, Marks, Roebuck and Rose for company.

Those festivals are finished now
But a certain summer holds me tight;
You at the front door keeping watch,
(Wondering whether Garner would be asked to bowl)
Turning with delight to say
"Blue skies over Clarence Park, Dad!"
In expectation of the day.

BIBLIOGRAPHY

Abram, Lawrence, 1974, Uphill and its Old Church
Arkwright Society, 1976 - 81, Weston-super-Mare Local History Trails 1 - 5
Austin, Brian,Tales of Old Weston, 1992/1993, Vols. 1 and 2
Bailey, John, 1986, Weston-super-Mare. Look back with Laughter
Barrett, J. H. 1978, A History of Maritime Forts in the Bristol Channel
Beisly, Philip, 1979, The Romantic Poets in the West Country
Beisly, Philip, 1988, Weston-super-Mare, a History and Guide
Beisly, Philip, 1996, The Northmarsh of Somerset
Bizley, Joyce, 1969, The Church of St. Martin, Worle
Bournville Past & Present Group, 1995, Yer tiz - Bournville Memories
Brown, Bryan and Loosley, John, 1979, The Book of Weston-super-Mare
Brown, Donald, 2006, Victoria's Uphill
Crockford-Hawley, John, 1990, A History of the Parish Church of All Saints
Crockford-Hawley, John, 2004, Weston-super-Mare, A History & Celebration
Dare and Frampton, 1888, A History of the Weston-super-Mare New Sea Front
Dymond, Charles W. 1902, Worlebury
Eddy, Andrew, 1983, The West Mendip Way
Evans, Jane, 1980, Worlebury. The Story of the Iron Age Fort
Farr, Grahame, 1954, Somerset Harbours
Harper, C.G. 1909, The Somerset Coast
Jackson, L.E.H & Rev. W. 1877, Visitors' Handbook to Weston-s-Mare
Jory, Bob, 1995, Flat Holm. Bristol Channel Island
Knight, F.A. 1902, The Sea-Board of Mendip
Lambert, David, 1998, Historic Public Parks, Weston-super-Mare
Legg, Rodney, 1983, The Steep Holm Guide
Legg, Rodney and Parsons, Tony, 1990, Steep Holm Wildlife
Moore, Gillian M. 1999, The Good Earth
Newman, Paul, 1976, Channel Passage
North Somerset Council, 2010, Weston-super-Mare's Seafront Enhancements
Overy, John and Robert, 1927, A Short History and Guide to the Weston District
Palmer, W.R. 1924, A Century of Weston-super-Mare History
Poole, Sharon, 1987, The Royal Potteries of Weston-super-Mare
Poole, Sharon, 1989, Around Weston-super-Mare in Old Photographs
Poole, Sharon, 1991, Weston-super-Mare in Old Photographs 1950s
Poole, Sharon, 2001, Weston-super-Mare 1950s - 1970s
Rendell, Stan & Joan, 1993, Steep Holm. The Story of a Small Island
Rendell, Stan & Joan, 2003, Steep Holm's Pioneers
Robbin's, 1899, Robbin's Guide to Weston-super-Mare
Rutter, John, 1829, Delineations of the North Western Division of the County of Somerset
Ryall, Sue, 1999, The Peoples' Village. Memories of Kewstoke
Simons, Grahame, 1988, Western Airways
Smith, Janet, 2005, Liquid Assets
Smith, Rosie and Howard, 2001, Weston-super-Mare in watercolours - an alternative guide
Terrell, Stan, 1993, Birnbeck Pier
Terrell, Stan, 2004, Milton and Worle
Tomalin, D. J. 1974, Woodspring Priory
Weston-super-Mare Civic Society, 1988, Uphill/Hutton Countryside Trails
Whittaker, A. and Green, G.W. 1983, Geology of the country around Weston-super-Mare
Willies, R.B. 1990, Westcliff - the Story of the School
Woodspring Museum 1979 Weston-super-Mare Anthology in Words and Pictures.
Woodspring Museum Service, 1995, Worlebury Hill
Worrall, D. H. and Surtees, P. R. 1984, Flat Holm

Other books by Rosie and Howard Smith:

Weston-super-Mare in watercolours - *an alternative guide*

West Somerset Coast in watercolours - *Brean to Porlock, a journey*

North Somerset Coast in watercolours - *Sand Bay to the Hotwells' Lock*

Somerset Hills in watercolours - *on higher ground*

Steep Holm Diary - *an island in the Bristol Channel*

www.garretpress.co.uk

In memoriam - the old Horse chestnut, Hutton

Weston-super-Mare
to the South

N

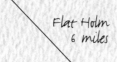

Flat Holm
6 miles

Steep Holm
5 miles

Fort

Brean Down

Black Rock

BREAN

River

no excuses for what's left out!